HAPPIER HUMANS

A 2020 VISION FOR AN INTEGRATED HEALTH
PROMOTION MODEL - FOR IMPROVED
PERSONAL, COMMUNITY, AND GLOBAL HEALTH

HUMANISM

ATHEISM

POSITIVITY

PERSONAL

IDEALS OF THE

ENLIGHTENMENT

RESPONSIBILITY

BY ANN NAIMISH, MPH, BSc

◆ FriesenPress

Suite 300 - 990 Fort St
Victoria, BC, V8V 3K2
Canada

www.friesenpress.com

ISBN
978-1-5255-6589-2 (Hardcover)
978-1-5255-6590-8 (Paperback)
978-1-5255-6591-5 (eBook)

1. philosophy, movements, humanism

Distributed to the trade by The Ingram Book Company

Disclaimer: this book is not meant to offend anyone, and the writer recognizes that some people will not agree with the content. I've attempted to the best of my abilities to put forth my vision in a respectful way.

TABLE OF CONTENTS

127   SECTION 4
SOME QUESTIONS TO ASK YOURSELF

FOREWORD

The content of this book has been percolating in my mind for the last 40 years. After working almost twenty years as a registered dietitian, public health nutrition specialist, university instructor and business owner, it became apparent that the way we as a society view health and health promotion is often very narrow. A lot of my previous jobs were educational, and I hope this book is as well. The health promotion concept has never been so important in the world as it is now. The Covid-19 pandemic illustrates perfectly how all humans on the earth are all connected. The countries that are handling the pandemic well are ones that have a very strong public health sector. In fact, this book will show that the healthiest populations are also the happiest, wealthiest, and the least religious. These same countries have a combination of capitalism and socialism (health and education systems), that support their people. Compassionate capitalism seems to work to both incentivize people to do their best and achieve their potential while still looking out and caring for the most vulnerable and marginalized communities in the world. We must make this world work for everyone, not just some select few.

Health is wealth! Without a very healthy population, a country cannot hope to improve its wealth and happiness. That is why it is so important not only to consider the individual, but also whole communities' and countries' health. In this book I provide evidence-based recommendations for strong public health and education systems as opposed to a for-profit model for health and education. I also stress the importance of allowing free markets to operate for increased economic innovation, efficiencies and wealth creation.

Why do I address and condemn religion in this book? Statistics show that the more religious a country or population, the less healthy the people. I go into this much more deeply later. Although correlation is not causation, there is excellent evidence to suggest that keeping religion out of the public sphere completely, correlates to much better health outcomes. Religion seems to be a taboo subject even in developed countries. Protected and shrouded, it seems to get a pass from many people. I argue that it should be assessed just as any other institution is. Finance, education, health systems – all are open to in-depth evaluation. I suggest that religious schools, churches and programs need to be held up to the same level of scrutiny if they are receiving tax breaks or public funds. Unfortunately, we continue to hear and see public figures such as politicians and educators speaking about their religion, religious views and how these might affect their policy decisions. Rather than simply illustrating all the negatives about religion, I provide an alternate moral philosophy. Humanism. It contains similar recurring morals as most religions (Judaism, Islam, Christianity, Hinduism) but without the god scam. Prior to evangelism, messiahs and prophets, humans had ancient Greek philosophers such as Socrates, Aristotle and Epicurus. Instead of humans continuing to rely on the Greeks' evidence, logic and reasoning, they turned towards the incredible pull of messianism (Jesus Christ) and prophets. In other words, instead of relying on Socratic and empirical methods (explained later in book), people flocked to the miracles, magical-thinking and unprovable afterlife of religion. We've now been suffering the consequences for 2000 years! It's time to put reason, rationalism and logic at the forefront of humanity if we are to make any progress as individuals, countries and as a world. Humanism fits perfectly with health promotion and progress because it is concerned with all humans on the globe.

A humanist world view has been extremely satisfactory in answering the questions: What guides you? What do you stand for? The following book is a **summary** of an integrated global, community, and personal health promotion vision I've created:

HAPPIER (humanism, atheism, positivity, personal responsibility, and contained within, the ideals of the enlightenment). I hope you enjoy the read.

INTRODUCTION

"As an atheist, I am angry that we live in a society in which the plain truth cannot be spoken without offending ninety percent of the population."
Sam Harris

GOALS OF THIS BOOK:

1. To present leadership and education about humanism, atheism, positivity, personal responsibility, and enlightenment ideals.

2. To influence (that is, increase) the numbers of people choosing humanism vs superstitious belief systems (god and religious systems).

3. To provide a workable health promotion model and vision for personal, community, and global human flourishing and growth/evolution.

This guidebook provides the reader with information on HAPPIER: Humanism, Atheism, Positivity, and Personal Responsibility, all underpinned with the ideals of the enlightenment (pluralism and tolerance). Practical techniques to incorporate into your life (PPR = positivity, personal responsibility) are found in the appendix. This guidebook was written for anyone with an interest in these topics, as well as learning about a new model to strive for a more contented life. It contains personal development and spirituality with a global outlook, so it can be taken as a life position or philosophy to live by.

Humanism is the starting point and is suggested as a replacement for traditional superstitious religious systems. Atheism is discussed, focusing on its benefits. These topics relate to the global and community levels and are blended with the PPR (positivity and personal responsibility) in the personal/individual level of the model.

Recognizing that everyone on the planet is interconnected and affected by the actions and beliefs of others—the starting point that could be the common foundation for *all* of humankind on the planet is: Humanism and Human Rights.

SECTION 1

HUMANISM AND HUMAN RIGHTS

Humanism is:

- A very positive, non-religious philosophy, life-stance, and world view based on liberal human values (tolerance of differences and plurality—many types of people living together).

- Recognizes that all humans have descended from a common African ancestor, so there is no race. Race is a social construct only. The ability to mate and produce offspring indicates humans are one species.

- Recognizes human rights across the globe.

- A common ground for all humans to start from (as opposed to differing religious beliefs).

- Is inclusive. Everyone in the world could be a humanist; the only condition is that you are a human being and agree with the following principles:

THE HUMANIST MANIFESTO III (2003)[1]

Knowledge of the world is derived by observation, experimentation, and rational analysis.

Humanists find that science is the best method for determining this knowledge as well as for solving problems and developing beneficial technologies. We also recognize the value of departures in thought, the arts, and inner experience—each is subject to analysis by critical intelligence.

Humans are an integral part of nature, the result of evolutionary change.

We accept our life as all and enough, distinguishing things as they are from things as we might wish or imagine them to be. We welcome the challenges of the future and are drawn to and undaunted by the yet to be known.

Ethical values are derived from human need and interest as tested by experience.

---

1   Pinker, Steven. Enlightenment Now. Penguin (reprint edition 2019) Pg. 410-411.

Humanists ground values in human welfare shaped by human circumstances, interests, and concerns, extended to the global ecosystem and beyond.

Life's fulfillment emerges from individual participation in the service of human ideals.

We animate our lives with a deep sense of purpose, finding wonder and awe in the joys and beauties of human existence, its challenges and tragedies, and even in the inevitability and finality of death.

Humans are social by nature and find meaning in relationships.

Humanists strive toward a world of mutual care and concern, free of cruelty and its consequences, where differences are resolved cooperatively without resorting to violence.

Working to benefit society maximizes individual happiness.

Progressive cultures have worked to free humanity from the brutalities of mere survival and to reduce suffering, improve society, and develop a global community.

Amsterdam Declaration 2002 (Humanists International) (the official defining statement of World Humanism)

Humanism is the outcome of a long tradition of free thought that has inspired many of the world's great thinkers and creative artists, and gave rise to science itself.

The fundamentals of modern Humanism are as follows:

1. Humanism is ethical. It affirms worth, dignity, and autonomy of the individual and the right of every human being to the greatest possible freedom compatible with the rights of others. Humanists have a duty of care to all of humanity including future generations. Humanists believe that morality is an intrinsic part of human nature based on understanding and a concern for others, needing no external sanction.

2. Humanism is rational. It seeks to use science creatively, not destructively. Humanists believe that the solutions to the world's problems lie in human thought and action rather than divine intervention. Humanism advocates the application of the methods of science and free inquiry to the problems of human welfare. But Humanists also believe that the application of science and technology must be tempered by human values. Science gives us the means, but human values must propose the ends.

3. Humanism supports democracy and human rights. Humanism aims at the fullest possible development of every human being. It holds that democracy and human development are matters of right. The principles of democracy and human rights can be applied to many human relationships and are not restricted to methods of government.

4. Humanism insists that personal liberty must be combined with social responsibility. Humanism ventures to build a world on the idea of the free person responsible to society, and recognises our dependence on and responsibility for the natural world. Humanism is undogmatic, imposing no creed upon its adherents. It is thus committed to education free from indoctrination.

5. Humanism is a response to the widespread demand for an alternative to dogmatic religion. The world's major religions claim to be based on revelations fixed for all time, and many seek to impose their world views on humanity. Humanism recognises that reliable knowledge of the world and ourselves arises through a continuing process of observation, evaluation, and revision.

6. Humanism values artistic creativity and imagination, and recognises the transforming power of art. Humanism affirms the importance of literature, music, and the visual and performing arts for personal development and fulfilment.

7. Humanism is a life-stance, aiming at the maximum possible fulfilment through the cultivation of ethical and creative living, and offers an ethical and rational means of addressing the challenges of our times. Humanism can be a way of life for everyone everywhere.

What is a humanistic good life?[2]

1. Meaningful and purposeful

2. Lived in relationships—love & friendship

3. Active in learning, making, and doing

4. Honest and authentic

5. Autonomous, in that each person is responsible for their own life choices

6. Feeling of satisfaction and contentedness

7. Integration of all of the above in working for the greater good of society

The Age of Reason and the Enlightenment were precursors to the development of English, French, and American statements of rights. The United Nations (UN) then developed the Universal Declaration of Human Rights (UDHR) (1948); later used in developing the International Bill of Human Rights (1966). In 1976, the International Covenant on Civil and Political Rights came into effect, providing legal (not just moral) obligations to most of the Declaration. The Declaration was a fundamental constitutive document of the UN, and formed the foundation for other human rights contracts. The UDHR (below) and the Humanist Manifesto can and should be foundational documents by which all country leaders can be guided. Idealist yes, but very worthwhile. As a review…

---

2   Grayling, A.C. *The God Argument*. Bloomsbury 2013. Pg.161-162.

THE UNITED NATIONS—UNIVERSAL DECLARATION OF HUMAN RIGHTS (1948) (UDHR)

Preamble (UN Charter)

We the peoples of the UN determined that

To save succeeding generations from the scourge of war, which twice in our lifetime has brought untold sorrow to mankind, and

To reaffirm faith in fundamental human rights, in the dignity and worth of the human person, in the equal rights of men and women and of nations large and small, and

To establish conditions under which justice and respect for the obligations arising from treaties and other sources of international law can be maintained, and

To promote social progress and better standards of life in larger freedom,

And for these ends

To practice tolerance and live together in peace with one another as good neighbors, and

To unite our strength to maintain international peace and security, and

To ensure, by the acceptance of principles and the institution of methods, that armed force shall not be used, save in the common interest, and

To employ international machinery for the promotion of the economic and social advancement of all peoples,

Have Resolved to Combine Our Efforts to Accomplish These Aims

Accordingly, our respective Governments, through representatives assembled in the city of San Francisco, who have exhibited their full powers found to be in good and due form, have agreed to the present Charter of the United Nations and do hereby establish an international organization to be known as the United Nations.

Adopted and Proclaimed by General Assembly Resolution 217 A (III) of 10 December 1948

Whereas recognition of the inherent dignity and of the equal and inalienable rights of all members of the human family is the foundation of freedom, justice, and peace in the world,

Whereas disregard and contempt for human rights have resulted in barbarous acts which have outraged the conscience of mankind, and the advent of a world in which human beings shall enjoy freedom of speech and belief and freedom from fear and want has been proclaimed as the highest aspiration of the common people,

Whereas it is essential, if man is not to be compelled to have recourse, as a last resort, to rebellion against tyranny and oppression, that human rights should be protected by the rule of law,

Whereas it is essential to promote the development of friendly relations between nations,

Whereas the peoples of the UN have in the Charter reaffirmed their faith in fundamental human rights, in the dignity and worth of the human person, and in the equal rights of men and women, and have determined to promote social progress and better standards of life in a larger freedom,

Whereas Member States have pledged themselves to achieve, in co-operation with the UN, the promotion of universal respect for and observance of human rights and fundamental freedoms,

Whereas a common understanding of these rights and freedoms is of the greatest importance for the full realization of this pledge,

(*) Voting: 48 for, including USA; 0 against; 8 abstentions (Eastern bloc, Saudi Arabia, and South Africa)

Now, therefore,

The General Assembly Proclaims this Universal Declaration of Human Rights as a common standard of achievement for all peoples and all nations, to the end that every individual and every organ of society, keeping this Declaration constantly in mind, shall strive by teaching and education to promote respect for these rights and freedoms and by progressive measures, national and international, to secure their universal and effective recognition and observance, both among the peoples of Member States themselves and among the peoples of territories under their jurisdiction.

Article 1

All human beings are born free and equal in dignity and rights. They are endowed with reason and conscience and should act toward one another in a spirit of brotherhood.

Article 2

Everyone is entitled to all the rights and freedoms set forth in this Declaration, without distinction of any kind, such as race, color, sex, language, religion, political or other opinion, national or social origin, property, birth, or other status.

Furthermore, no distinction shall be made on the basis of the political, jurisdictional, or international status of the country or territory to which a person belongs, whether it be independent, trust, non-self-governing, or under any other limitation of sovereignty.

Article 3

Everyone has the right to life, liberty, and security of person.

Article 4

No one shall be held in slavery or servitude; slavery and the slave trade shall be prohibited in all their forms.

Article 5

No one shall be subjected to torture or to cruel, inhuman, or degrading treatment or punishment.

Article 6

Everyone has the right to recognition everywhere as a person before the law.

Article 7

All are equal before the law and are entitled without any discrimination to equal protection of the law. All are entitled to equal protection against any discrimination in violation of this Declaration and against any incitement to such discrimination.

Article 8

Everyone has the right to an effective remedy by the competent national tribunals for acts violating the fundamental rights granted him by the constitution or by law.

Article 9

No one shall be subjected to arbitrary arrest, detention, or exile.

Article 10

Everyone is entitled in full equality to a fair and public hearing by an independent and impartial tribunal, in the determination of his rights and obligations and of any criminal charge against him.

Article 11

(1) Everyone charged with a penal offence has the right to be presumed innocent until proved guilty according to law in a public trial at which he has had all the guarantees necessary for his defense.

(2) No one shall be held guilty of any penal offence on account of any act or omission which did not constitute a penal offence, under national or international law, at the time when it was committed. Nor shall a heavier penalty be imposed than the one that was applicable at the time the penal offense was committed.

Article 12

No one shall be subjected to arbitrary interference with his privacy, family, home, or correspondence, nor to attacks upon his honor and reputation. Everyone has the right to the protection of the law against such interference or attacks.

Article 13

(1) Everyone has the right to freedom of movement and residence within the borders of each state

(2) Everyone has the right to leave any country, including his own, and to return to his country.

Article 14

(1) Everyone has the right to seek and to enjoy in other countries asylum from persecution.

(2) This right may not be invoked in the case of prosecutions genuinely arising from non-political crimes or from acts contrary to the purposes and principles of the UN.

Article 15

(1) Everyone has a right to a nationality.

(2) No one shall be arbitrarily deprived of his nationality nor denied the right to change his nationality.

Article 16

(1) Men and women of full age, without any limitation due to race, nationality or religion, have the right to marry and to found a family. They are entitled to equal rights as to marriage, during marriage and at its dissolution.

(2) Marriage shall be entered into only with the free and full consent of the intending spouses.

(3) The family is the natural and fundamental group unit of society and is entitled to protection by society and the State.

Article 17

(1) Everyone has the right to own property alone as well as in association with others.

(2) No one shall be arbitrarily deprived of his property.

Article 18

Everyone has the right to freedom of thought, conscience, and religion; this right includes freedom to change his religion or belief, and freedom, either alone or in community with others and in public or private, to manifest his religion in teaching, practice, worship, and observance.

Article 19

Everyone has the right to freedom of opinion and expression; this right includes freedom to hold opinions without interference and to seek, receive and impart information and ideas through any media and regardless of frontiers.

Article 20

(1) Everyone has the right to freedom of peaceful assembly and association.

(2) No one may be compelled to belong to an association.

Article 21

(1) Everyone has the right to take part in the government of his country, directly or through freely chosen representatives.

(2) Everyone has the right of equal access to public service in his country.

(3) The will of the people shall be the basis of the authority of government; this will shall be expressed in periodic and genuine elections which shall be by universal and equal suffrage and shall be held by secret vote or by equivalent free voting procedures.

Article 22

Everyone, as a member of society, has the right to social security and is entitled to realization, through national effort and international co-operation and in accordance with the organization and resources of each State, of the economic, social, and cultural rights indispensable for his dignity and the free development of his personality.

Article 23

(1) Everyone has the right to work, to free choice of employment, to just and favorable conditions of work, and to protection against unemployment.

(2) Everyone, without any discrimination, has the right to equal pay for equal work.

(3) Everyone who works has the right to just and favorable remuneration ensuring for himself and his family an existence worthy of human dignity, and supplemented, if necessary, by other means of social protection.

(4) Everyone has the right to form and to join trade unions for the protection of his interests.

Article 24

Everyone has the right to rest and leisure, including reasonable limitation of working hours and periodic holidays with pay.

Article 25

(1) Everyone has the right to a standard of living adequate for the health and well-being of himself and his family, including food, clothing, housing, and medical care and necessary social services, and the right to security in the event of unemployment, sickness, disability, widowhood, old age, or other lack of livelihood in circumstances beyond his control.

(2) Motherhood and childhood are entitled to special care and assistance. All children, whether born in or out of wedlock, shall enjoy the same social protection.

Article 26

(1) Everyone has the right to education. Education shall be free, at least in the elementary and fundamental stages. Elementary education shall be compulsory. Technical

and professional education shall be made generally available and higher education shall be equally accessible to all on the basis of merit.

(2) Education shall be directed to the full development of the human personality and to the strengthening of respect for human rights and fundamental freedoms. It shall promote understanding, tolerance, and friendship among all nations, racial or religious groups, and shall further the activities of the UN for the maintenance of peace.

(3) Parents have a prior right to choose the kind of education that shall be given to their children.

Article 27

(1) Everyone has the right freely to participate in the cultural life of the community, to enjoy the arts and to share in scientific advancement and its benefits.

(2) Everyone has the right to the protection of the moral and material interests resulting from any scientific, literary, or artistic production of which he is the author.

Article 28

Everyone is entitled to a social and international order in which the rights and freedoms set forth in this Declaration can be fully realized.

Article 29

(1) Everyone has duties to the community in which alone the free and full development of his personality is possible.

(2) In the exercise of his rights and freedoms, everyone shall be subject only to such limitations as are determined by law, solely for the purpose of securing due recognition and respect for the rights and freedoms of others and of meeting the just requirements of morality, public order, and the general welfare in a democratic society.

(3) These rights and freedoms may in no case be exercised contrary to the purposes and principles of the UN.

Article 30

Nothing in this Declaration may be interpreted as implying for any State, group, or person any right to engage in any activity or to perform any act aimed at the destruction of any of the rights and freedoms set forth herein.

SECTION 2

ATHEISM
(BELIEF THERE IS NO GOD)

Many people wonder why a person would choose atheism over a religious belief system. If a person reads the entire Bible, the Torah, or the Koran, they might find the many stories of extreme violence, torture, rape, misogyny, and racism very easy to reject. Exact numbers of atheists/non-religious/secularists are hard to find because measurement methodology of this statistic is not consistent, and admitting to atheism is illegal and/or highly stigmatized in some countries. Numbers of non-believers are likely higher for this reason. According to Pew Research, Global Religions Landscape, 2012, Scandinavian countries have a very low rate of god belief—around 30% believe, 70% don't believe; the USA has about 80% believers, and only 20% non-believers, and Canada is in between, with about 70% believers and 30%

non-believers. In the same report, the religiously unaffiliated comprise 76% of the Czech Republic. More non-religious numbers are: North Korea, 71%, Estonia 60%, Japan 57%, Hong Kong 56%, and China 52%. Pew Research Centre, also 2012, surveyed 230 countries *across the globe* and found that 16% of people were not affiliated with any religion while 84% were. This can be explained by the fact that in some countries such as Iran, Saudi Arabia, and Pakistan, the total number of believers is close to 100% (reported), and they have large populations, as do India and Africa, where God belief is also very high. The countries where God belief is quite low have very small populations in comparison. Birth rates and fertility are highest in the most religious countries so in absolute numbers, religiosity is increasing in the world.

It is easy to understand why people believe in God—especially people who have not had the good fortune to receive a higher education, particularly in the sciences. It is also understandable that when children are immersed and brainwashed in superstitious myths, they grow up to believe them. They simply have not learned anything different. In this book, I promote the Big Bang theory and the theory of evolution as the best explanations for the creation of the universe and the evolution of life on earth. More explanation of the Big Bang is given in the glossary.

Culture and tradition continue to pass on tribal stories meant for illiterate, tribal peoples. Bible stories, as well as those from the Koran and Torah contain many fables that promote the idea of divisiveness, exclusivity, war, rape, misogyny, and violence. When people are identified by their religion, it is inherently divisive and negative, even though that may not be the intent. In the twenty-first century, continuing to identify as Christian, Muslim, Jewish etc., serves to promote ongoing conflicts, war, repression, and regressive ways of thinking. To move forward as humankind, with a global interest, we need to move past these superstitious, backward ways of thinking. By choosing atheism, which is a belief in no god/supernatural being(s), we can choose humanism and human rights, which could bring together all of humankind, not just a subset of humans (as religions do).

BENEFITS OF ATHEISM[3,4]

- It is absolutely false that atheists "don't believe in anything". This is simply *not true*. Atheists believe that we alone as one human being and as a collective of human beings, can create and determine how we live

---

3   McGreal, S.A. *Religiosity, Atheism and Health: The Atheist Advantage.* Psychology Today, March, 2019.

4   Galen, L. *Atheism, Wellbeing, and the Wager: Why Not Believing in God (With Others) is Good for You. Science, Religion and Culture.* 2(3):54-69. 2015.

life—eliminating the delusion that there is a benevolent "Father in Heaven," and that there is an afterlife.

- Atheism is an evolution of mankind growing up from a child-like state where a god takes care of us; a realization and final rejection of myths and superstitions.

- Realization that we have agency and are personally responsible for our lives and our world.

- Realization that we should make the best of this life, as this is all we get.

- Realization that we can choose how to create meaning in our lives and how we want to be spiritual.

Secular people tend to share these traits[5],[6]:

- Thinking for themselves

- Self-reliance, while realizing interdependence with others

- Freedom of thought and speech

- Intellectual inquiry

- Pragmatic problem solving

- Cultivating independence in children

- Pursuing truth, justice, and freedom

- Accepting death as a natural part of the life cycle

5   Zuckerman, Phil. *Living the Secular Life*. 2014 .

6   Dutton, E. & Van derLinden. *Why is Intelligence Negatively Associated with Religiousness?* Evolutionary Psychological Science. 2017. DOI: 10.1007/s40806-017-0101-0.

- Sober pragmatism grounded in this world (not the non-existent next)
- Tend to be more tolerant
- Against torture
- Against military action
- Care more about earth
- More supportive of LGBTQs
- More supportive of women's reproductive rights
- Lower levels of incarceration

According to Paul Kurtz, a great American secularist:

- Most secularists believe that science and education enhance life
- Democracy and respect for human rights are essential elements of a good society
- Justice and fairness are ideals to strive for
- The earth is to be valued and protected
- Honesty, decency, tolerance, integrity, love, altruism, and self-responsibility are ideals
- Creative and artistic expression are vital parts of human existence
- Life is intrinsically beautiful, wonderful, and sublime (no need to ruin it with religion)

- Wonder and transcendence can be experienced in nature, meditation, art, dance, deep involvement in one's work (getting into the flow zone), humanitarianism, volunteer work.

Compare the previous points to Superstitious/ Supernatural/Religious Phenomena and Beliefs[7] In:

- God, gods, deities, spirits, ghosts, auras, souls
- Crystals, rocks attributed to having certain powers, holy water, holy oil
- Tarot cards, seers, fortune tellers
- Magic, miracles, astrology
- Unicorns, fairies, elves, goblins
- Monsters, jade eggs, pixie dust
- Santa Claus, Easter Bunny, Superman, Tooth Fairy

Profile of most religious (Zuckerman, P.):

- Tend to be more racist
- Support death penalty
- In favor of torture
- More militaristic
- Higher incarceration rates

---

7   Palermo, E. *The Origins of Religion: How Supernatural Beliefs Evolved.* Livescience.com. October 5, 2015.

- Tend to be less educated

- Tend not to think for themselves as much as secularists

- Tend to be poorer

HAPPIER MORALITY CODE, VIRTUES, AND VALUES

Some people believe that atheists cannot be good people. They drank the sugary drinks that were given to them in childhood by well-meaning god-believers. They were taught as children that morality comes from a belief in God. *This is simply wrong.* Humans have an inborn sense of goodness and rightness as well as a fighting/warring side. To survive as a species, we had to evolve socially accepted behavior codes. We have innate moral codes. In fact, generally religions are very negative in their view of humans as sinners and wrongdoers. I prefer to say that all humans make mistakes, and that is ok. We are human (animals), *not* perfect. We can strive to be our best selves, but we don't need religions to do this. We don't need all the negativity, violence, misogyny, and nonsense contained in the holy books. It all comes down to one simple, main idea captured by:

The Golden, Silver, and Platinum Rules

(The earliest version was written about 624 BCE in Thales, Greece); Egyptians wrote it, too (600 BCE), as did Confucius (500 BCE).

- Do unto others as you would have done to yourself.

- Treat others as you'd like to be treated.

- It's good to do and be good.

This is pretty much it. *Straight and simple.* Not full of hellfire (Bible) or promises of virgins (Koran) in a non-existent heaven. Nothing about complicated myths and fables full of horror meant to scare people into submission.

Morals summary

- Be a good person. How?
- First, do no harm to others.
- Be kind.
- Try to help others (empathetic reciprocity). Most of us have this inbuilt and wired into our brains; when we help others, we feel good as well—it's mutually beneficial.

How is basic human empathy developed?

- People learn from a young age by observing and experiencing.
- Socialization in schools, at home and in the community.
- The basic code of conduct of human decency requires no outdated Bible stories.

Seven generally accepted Moral Principles found across all cultures include[8]:

1. Love your family

2. Help your group

3. Return favours

4. Be brave

5. Defer to authority

6. Be fair

7. Respect others' property

Moral Codes can be expanded to include:

-   Autonomy (self-rule; respecting each person has the right to make their own decisions)

-   Beneficence = doing good

-   Nonmaleficence = do no harm

-   Honesty=free from lies and deceit

-   Be forgiving

-   Be responsible for your actions (Fidelity = loyalty, fulfilling your commitments)

-   Be tolerant of differences

-   Be humble

---

8   Curry, O.S. University of Oxford. *Morals Project*. *Kindness.org*, professor in the Philosophy of Natural and Social Sciences, London School of Economics.

-   Be generous

Humanist Virtues

-   Courage
-   Cognition/Knowledge
-   Caring

Humanist Values Summary

-   Honesty
-   Reason
-   Critical Thinking
-   Cooperation in every facet of human interdependence
-   Democracy
-   Rule of Law

NON-RELIGIOUS WAYS TO GET INSPIRATION, HOPE, AND CONNECTION (SPIRITUALITY)

Realize that you can create your own spirituality, traditions, rituals, and experiences to replace any religious ones you may have been used to.

Some ideas:

-   Your work—getting into an area that you believe in and feel you can make a difference in

- Nature—hiking, biking, water sports; Darwin day, Earth day, summer solstice, vernal equinox
- Music—choirs, bands, playing/learning an instrument, going to concerts
- Drama, theatre and dance—watching and/or participating in performances of all types
- Art—galleries, museums, classes, tours—watch/create/participate
- Cinema, movies
- Literature—book clubs, library, reading, writing
- Sports clubs
- Community and charity clubs (Rotary, Shriners, Lions)
- Volunteering at any of the above
- Dinner and travel clubs

> *"Work gives you meaning and purpose in life and life is empty without it."*
> Stephen Hawking

Summary of **HAPPIER** Morality Code

All of us must think for ourselves; religions do not want you to do this; they just want you to follow their doctrines.

At the most basic level of godlessness—it means humans have to actively, in their own minds, choose how to treat others.

Leaving these decisions up to a god to tell us how to behave, is a complete cop-out of our basic human ethical duty.

The closer we are to giving authority to a god, the more we become vulnerable to manipulation by authority figures, which can result in decreasing levels of democracy.

We must also be active participants in making changes; passive attitudes such as "victim of circumstance" do not help anyone (we need to take personal responsibility for our lives). The root meaning of heresy = hairesis (Greek) = choice. We all have choice in how to respond to our circumstances.

The world has changed immensely in the last two thousand years. Old systems need major revisions. In fact, just reforming old religious systems is not enough. The expiry date of superstitious belief systems has passed. Religious systems need to be demoted completely if we are to evolve as a *global human community with mutual care and respect.* Learning lessons from history when religious systems were dominant is necessary. Indeed, they did inform our legal, educational, and cultural systems. But now that we have international human rights, legal/judicial and scientific systems to more objectively judge facts and evidence, religious systems are no longer necessary. In fact, they are regressive, holding us back from better ways to live in harmony within the world. We have democracy and the rule of law, and even though these are far from perfect, they are generally regarded as the optimal way of governing. We need to move completely away from superstition, mysticism, and religion if we on the planet have any chance of decreasing conflicts, wars, bigotry, and hatred. The next section will outline some of the notable historical figures who were atheists/skeptics. After that, the major reasons for my statements above are discussed in "Problems with Religion."

SOME FAMOUS SKEPTICS, SECULARISTS AND ATHEISTS

Xenophanes (570-480 BCE) – Greek philosopher, poet, and theologian. Satirized traditional religious views as "human projections." Used evidence of fossils to show that water must have covered the earth originally.

Protagoras (490-420 BCE) – Greek philosopher. "Concerning the gods, I have no means of knowing whether they exist, nor of what sort they may be, because of the obscurity of the subject, and the brevity of human life." "Man is the measure of all things."

Socrates (470-399 BCE) – Greek philosopher. Founder of the first school of higher learning "The Academy." Ethics or moral philosophy is a branch of philosophy that involves systematizing, defending, and recommending concepts of right and wrong. One of his students was Plato. The Socratic method is the process of critical thinking/analysis.

Aristophanes (448-380 BCE) – Greek writer and intellectual. "Shrines! Shrines! Surely you don't believe in the gods. What's your argument? Where's your proof?" "Open your mouth and shut your eyes, and see what Zeus shall send you." Considered one of the best playwrights of comedies in history.

Aristotle (384-322 BCE) – Greek philosopher and scientist. "Men create gods in their own image not only with regard to their form, but their mode of life."

Epicurus (341-270 BCE) – Greek philosopher. "Fabulous persuasion in faith is the approbation of feigned ideas or notions; it is credulous belief in the reality of phantoms."

Seneca (4BCE-65AD) – Roman philosopher and tutor/advisor to Nero. Proponent of the Stoic's philosophy of self-mastery "Of Peace of Mind," "On Mercy," "On the Happy Life."

Frances Bacon (1561-1626 AD) – UK, High Lord Chancellor of England and Attorney General of England and Wales. His works are credited with developing the scientific method—father of "empiricism."

Thomas Hobbes (1588-1679) - UK, philosopher. Wrote book *Leviathan* (social contract theory), classical realism.

Pierre Bayle (1647-1706) - French Calvinist. Known for *Historical and Critical Dictionary*, philosophical skepticism, known for "toleration—a fair, objective, and permissive attitude toward those whose opinions, beliefs, and practices, racial or ethnic origins differ from one's own."

Jean Meslier (1664-1729) - French Catholic priest who upon his death was found to have written essays denouncing all religions as false and promoting atheism and materialism.

David Hume (1711-1776) – Scottish. Philosophical empiricism, scepticism and naturalism; wrote *A Treatise of Human Nature*.

Diderot (1713-1784) - French philosopher, art critic, and writer. *The Skeptic's Walk*; *On the Interpretation of Nature*.

Baron d'Holbach (1723- 1776) – French. *The System of Nature*. Figured prominently in the French Enlightenment.

Voltaire (1694-1778) – French writer. "Common sense is not so common," "those who can make you believe absurdities can make you commit atrocities," "God is a comedian playing to an audience too afraid to laugh."

Thomas Jefferson (1743-1826) – Founding father, second vice-president, and third president of the USA. Principal author of the Declaration of Independence, a proponent of democracy, republicanism, and individual rights.

Abraham Lincoln (1809-1865) - Sixteenth president of the USA. Abolished slavery.

Susan B. Anthony (1820-1906) - American social reformer. Played a pivotal role in women's suffrage, and a key role in creating the International Council of Women.

Thomas Edison (1847-1931) - American businessman and inventor (long-burning light bulb, phonograph, motion picture camera). He had huge impact on the modern industrialized world; he was a "freethinker"—"Nature is what we know. We do not know the gods of religions. And nature is not kind, or merciful, or loving. If God made me—the fabled God of the three qualities of which I spoke—mercy, kindness, love—He also made the fish I catch and eat. And where do His mercy, kindness, and love for that fish come in? No, nature made us—nature did it all—not the gods of the religions."

Charles Darwin (1809-1882) - English naturalist. Science of evolution (common ancestors), natural selection, wrote *On the Origin of Species, The Descent of Man.*

Friedrich Nietzsche (1844-1900) - German philosopher, scholar, cultural critic. "To live is to suffer, to survive is to find some meaning in the suffering" "The Death of God"—meaning, figuratively, that the Enlightenment had killed the possibility of belief in God or any gods having ever existed. Some of his works include *Beyond Good and Evil, The Antichrist, The Will to Power.*

Sigmund Freud (1856-1939) - German/Austrian neurologist, founder of psychoanalysis; dreams analysis; model of id, ego, and super-ego. Regarded God as an illusion based on the child-like need for a strong "father." He maintained that religion in modern times could be set aside. *Obsessive Actions and Religious Practices* (1907) notes the likeness between religious belief and neurotic behaviour. Argued that the belief of a supernatural protector serves as consolation for "man's fear of death and for an afterlife." Religion can be explained by its function in society, not in its relation to truth. That is why religions are illusions, according to Freud.

Mark Twain (1835-1910) - Real name, Samuel Langhorne Clemens - American humorist, writer, publisher, and lecturer. Wrote *Tom Sawyer* and *Huckleberry Finn*. "Faith is believing what you know ain't so." "If Christ was here now there is one thing he wouldn't be—a Christian."

Bertrand Russell (1872-1970) - British philosopher, logician, mathematician, writer, historian, social critic. *Principa Mathematica*; anti-war, anti-imperialism, champion of humanitarian ideals and freedom of thought, maintained religion to be nothing more than superstition, member of Advisory Council of the British Humanist Association.

Albert Einstein (1879-1955) - German-born theoretical physicist who developed the theory of relativity, one of the two pillars of modern physics (alongside quantum mechanics). Originated $E=mc^2$.

H. L. Mencken (1880-1956) - American journalist, cultural critic, satirist, and scholar; outspoken critic of organized religion, belief in god(s), populism.

Julian Huxley (1887-1975) - UK, evolutionary biologist, internationalist, first president of the British Humanist Association. Brother of writer Aldous Huxley, involved in the creation of the United Nations Educational, Scientific and Cultural Organization (UNESCO); known for his idea of promoting birth control to limit population growth; one of the signers of the Humanist Manifesto; *Religion without Revelation*, *Essays of a Humanist*, *The Future of Man*.

Jean-Paul Sartre (1905-1980) - French philosopher noted for existentialism and phenomenology; *Being and Nothingness*, *Existentialism Is a Humanism*, *The Age of Reason*.

Simone de Beauvoir (1908-1986) - French feminist existentialist and philosopher. *The Second Sex*; *The Ethics of Ambiguity*.

Albert Camus (1913-1960) - French writer and philosopher. *The Stranger*, *The Myth of Sisyphus*; *The Rebel*; *The Plague*; known for absurdism, "life is absurd—humans should still strive to find meaning and purpose in life."

Richard Feynman (1918-1988) - American theoretical physicist, Nobel Prize in physics in 1965; Cal-Tech professor, very famous scientist. Assisted in the development of the atomic bomb during WWII, and investigated Space Shuttle Challenger disaster (1986). Known for quantum computing, nanotechnology, wrote *The Feynman Lectures on Physics*, *Surely You're Joking, Mr. Feynman*, *What Do You Care What Other People Think?* Biographies and movies (*Infinity*, *QED*) opera, too many accolades to list.

Isaac Asimov (1920-1992) - American Professor of Biochemistry (Boston University). Prolific writer of science fiction, mystery, and popular and hard science; served as president of the American Humanist Association (AHA); founding member of the Committee for the Scientific Investigation of Claims of the Paranormal (now the Committee for Skeptical Inquiry); *The Robot Series*, *Galactic Empire* novels, *Foundation* prequels, original *Foundation* trilogy, extended *Foundation* series, *Lucky Star* series, *Norby Chronicles*, "Three Laws of Robotics," coined the term "robotics," *The Intelligent Man's Guide to Science*; *The Humanist Way*, *In Pursuit of Truth*, too many awards to list.

Kurt Vonnegut (1922-2007) - American writer, *Slaughterhouse Five*, *Bluebeard*, and many more.

Carl Sagan (1934-1996) - Professor of Astronomy at Cornell University, American astrophysicist, astrobiologist, astronomer, cosmologist, author, prolific science writer; amazing discovery, by experiment, of the production of amino acids from basic chemicals by radiation; best known for his research on extraterrestrial life; *The Dragons of Eden, Pale Blue Dot, Cosmos* (TV series and book); too many awards to list.

Prabir Ghosh (1945–) - Indian writer. Founder and president of a science and rationalists' association based in Kolkata, India.

Kip Thorne (1940–) – American. theoretical physicist. Cal-Tech professor, author and filmmaker; *Interstellar* (film), *Gravitation* (book); too many scientific prizes to mention.

Christopher Hitchens (1949-2011) - British/USA author and social critic. "All religions are false, harmful, and authoritarian." Argued in favour of free expression and scientific discovery, and that it was superior to religion as an ethical code of conduct for human civilization. Hitchen's razor = "What can be asserted without evidence, can be dismissed without evidence." "Religion is: "violent, irrational, intolerant, allied to racism, tribalism, and bigotry, invested in ignorance, and hostile to free inquiry, contemptuous of women and children: (it) ought to have a great deal on its conscience." Hitchens said humanity is in need of a renewed Enlightenment. He stated that one of the most unfortunate moments in human history was the revolt of the Maccabeans due to the reversion from Hellenistic thought and philosophy to messianism and fundamentalism.

Victor Stenger (1935-2014) - American particle physicist, author, philosopher, and religious skeptic. Wrote *God: the Failed Hypothesis. How Science Shows that God Does Not Exist*. He was an advocate for removing the influence of religion from scientific research, commercial activity, and the political process. He was a prominent critic of intelligent design; he criticized those who invoke the perplexities of quantum mechanics in support of the paranormal, mysticism, or supernatural phenomenon.

Stephen Hawking (1942-2018) - English theoretical physicist and author. Director of Centre for Theoretical Cosmology, University of Cambridge (at his death); former Lucasian Professor of Mathematics at Cambridge; known for "Hawking radiation," *A Brief History of Time*; general relativity, quantum gravity; properties of expanding universes. Despite living with ALS for fifty years, he was able to communicate by using a specially adapted device. He stated: "There is a fundamental difference between religion, which is based on authority, and science, which is based on observation and reason. Science will win because it works." The conception of an afterlife he called "a fairy story for people afraid of the dark." "We are each free to believe what we want, and it is my view that there is no God. No one created the universe, and no one directs our fate."

"Before we understand science, it is natural to believe that God created the universe. But now science offers a more convincing explanation."

Richard Dawkins (1941–) - English evolutionary biologist, author, professor University of Oxford. Advocacy of evolutionism, critic of religion. Books include *The Selfish Gene, The Extended Phenotype, The Blind Watchmaker, The God Delusion.* Introduced the term "meme;" well-known for his criticism of creationism and intelligent design. Contends religious faith is a delusion.

Daniel Dennett (1942–) - American philosopher, professor at Tufts University, writer and cognitive scientist (evolutionary biology). Known for *Consciousness Explained, Darwin's Dangerous Idea, Breaking the Spell.*

A. C. Grayling (1949–) - British philosopher and author. Known for criticisms of arguments for God's existence. Vice-president of Humanists, UK., author of multiple books including *The God Argument: The Case Against Religion and For Humanism.*

William Henry III (Bill) Gates (1955 –) - American business magnate. Principal founder of Microsoft Corporation, investor, philanthropist, humanitarian. Runs the Gates Charitable Foundation with his wife Melinda. Involved with global health initiatives, including polio eradication and sewage and sanitation treatment in developing countries, among many global health initiatives.

Maryam Namazie (1966–) - Persian-British secularist and human rights activist. Commentator and broadcaster; ex-Muslim; Manifesto: Together Facing the New Totalitarianism (one of 12 signatories). The manifesto starts as follows: "After having overcome fascism, Nazism, and Stalinism, the world now faces a new totalitarian global threat: Islamism."

Sam Harris (1967–) - American public intellectual, author, cognitive neuroscientist, philosopher. Critic of religion, especially *Islam*; *The End of Faith*; *The Moral Landscape*; *Waking Up—a Guide to Spirituality Without Religion*; He promotes analysis of personal convictions compared to evidence, and where intellectual honesty is demanded equally in religious views and nonreligious views. He states that spirituality should be understood in light of scientific disciplines like neuroscience and psychology. Science, he contends, can show humans how to maximize well-being. Encourages secular meditation practice.

*Note: HA**PP**IE**R***

Positivity and Personal Responsibility topics are covered in the Appendix.

IDEALS OF THE ENLIGHTENMENT[9]

Included throughout this book, and in Humanism and Human Rights statements:

- All humans are equal; the *individual* is primary

- Importance of reason (science)

- Progress (meaning trying to improve present and future as opposed to staying in past traditions)

- Separation of church and state

- Government by the people for the people

- Plurality (many different peoples living together)

- Tolerance of differences

---

9   Pinker, Steven. *Enlightenment Now*. 2019.

SECTION 3

PROBLEMS WITH RELIGION

RELIGION AS DELUSIONAL THINKING[10]

The first premise (the personal level): The majority of humans live parts of their lives in delusion. When we look at the prevalence of preventable chronic diseases, indebtedness, and mental/emotional problems in most societies, clearly there are problems. Most of us have personal blind spots in different areas of our lives. This is very normal, expected, and understandable. Even though we know we should eat healthfully and exercise regularly, something hinders us. We know we should live within our means, but credit cards are so easy to use. We know we are carrying old family issues into our current relationships, but we seem unable to make changes. These can be mostly explained

---

10 Burnett, D. *The Idiot Brain: A Neuroscientist Explains What Your Head Is Really Up To*. Norton. 2016.

by the fact that humans will go for the easiest and most satisfying choices in the short term. Often that choice is simply ignoring or denying the issue (forms of self-delusion). Most people would love a magic pill to immediately solve their problems. The hard truth is that there are no magic pills.

The reality is that humans are susceptible to all sorts of manipulations from outside influences (marketing, social group, social media) but *mostly from our own brains11,12*. Our brains can trick us into believing we are right, even when we really are not. We can absolutely feel certain about something, but there's a good chance we're wrong. (see "Q & A—Did you know?" section for more explanation). Religion is a perfect example of people feeling sure of something (the existence of God) when evidence shows the opposite. Religion is a manipulative and delusional system. What do I mean by religion deluding us? We are deluding ourselves when we attest to a belief in god. By saying "I believe in God"—we are actively lying to ourselves, as there is no evidence of a god/gods ever existing in reality. There is no sugar-coating this truth. This must be very disappointing to the god-believers, but as adults (and children) we deserve honesty and truth. When many of our great scientists and thinkers are/have been skeptics/atheists, because they have never been able

---

11   Ambrosino, B. *Do humans have a 'religion instinct'?* and *How and why did religion evolve?* BBC Future. 2019.

12   Kahneman, D. *Thinking Fast and Slow*. Giroux. 2011.

to prove a god's existence in all of history, I believe them. The burden of proof is on the god believers and they have never in history been able to prove any god exists.

Who should we believe about the existence of a god? Steven Hawking, Kip Thorne, Victor Stenger, Lawrence Krauss, Jerry Coyne, Richard Dawkins, Christopher Hitchens, A. C. Grayling, Daniel Dennett, Sam Harris (some of the greatest minds in recent times) or Gwyneth Paltrow, Madonna, or Shirley MacLaine? Sorry to them—it's nothing personal—but they spew quackery all over the place. An entertainer (which is what a priest, preacher, rabbi is as well), is not qualified or trained to know how to evaluate scientific evidence. They are experienced in performing, entertaining, and telling stories.

Listen to the best scientists who have dedicated their lives to studying complex science, and not to a priest/preacher/minister/entertainer who can talk about myths from ancient Bibles/Torah/Koran, written 2000 years ago for illiterate, tribal people. Bill Gates is not going to hire Gwyneth Paltrow—he's going to hire the best engineers and scientists to find solutions to real problems. We can distract ourselves with consuming fun products and services from entertainers and that is not a problem—where the problems enter is if we believe some of the claims they are selling. For example, some of the health claims, mysticism, and reincarnation stories that have been promoted by these entertainers are simply wrong and ridiculous (and this includes the priests, preachers, rabbis).

Humans are prone to idolize sports stars and celebrities, but if we look at life-changing contributions from different types of people, should we not give much more credit to scientists, inventors, and educators? Not to negate the importance of entertainment in any way—it is very beneficial for just that—entertainment (feeling/emotional, brain engaged). When we look at religious saviours/idols/prophets—how do we *really* know the truth about Jesus, Mohammed, Abraham, Moses? Humans constructed myths/religious systems to fit their needs. There is evidence that these people existed, but the stories after thousands of years surely cannot be relied on as truth. There are some very exceptional people, but generally every human is simply human with human faults and weaknesses. It's impossible to believe that these people were much different from other humans, other than the fact that people are drawn to charismatic leaders and are prone to attribute idol status to them. The messages they were promoting were irresistible.

For his time, Jesus spoke of new ideas that gave the poor and miserable people hope. That hope was to be found in a (non-existing, but apparently incredible) after-life (heaven). The salvation and amazing after-life gave people the ultimate consolation of something to look forward to as their current life was so wretched. This was an incredibly sellable message. Of course, a life after death and heaven could not be proven, but it didn't matter. What mattered was that people seized the idea as it made them *feel* better. From the previous ancient master-slave mentality, to the idea that *all people* including the slaves, could have a better after-life, the idea was transformative for mankind's history. It began a way of thinking that did change the world—that a messiah was coming (again not provable), and that everyone could "go to heaven" if they followed God's rules. As an evolutionary phase in human development it made, and makes, complete sense. However, now 2000 years later, many countries have adopted human rights for all people, so believing in a false after-life is *not necessary*. Judeo-Christian history has informed our current legal/government and education systems, which needs to be acknowledged and understood, but now we can leave the outdated superstitions of "after-life" and "heaven" behind.

This god-belief delusion is also somewhat about risk-assessment. Our educators need to do a better job in teaching basic statistics and math to young people. The odds are extremely high there is no god. There has never been any *credible* evidence to prove there is a god. In other words, the probability that there is no god is extremely high. People have to ask themselves if they are willing to take the risk of severe disappointment at the end of their lives when they realize they are going nowhere except into the kiln or casket. When they finally realize that most of their prayers have gone unanswered, and they question whether there is a heaven, it could be extremely disappointing. Some will go to their death still believing in their imagination that they are going to heaven and to state it bluntly, ignorance is bliss. To think people have been manipulated and fooled by a religious system for a long time is a very sad and sorry prospect indeed. That is reality. Re-incarnation is a myth, a lie, and a magical wish that goes completely against reason. However, if a person believes that reincarnation means that a body decomposes into basic elements within the soil, and then is used to grow vegetables, trees or grass, then yes, this is reincarnation.

Promoting the idea of a "rebirth" if one acts properly according to God is also a myth. It may be an ideal to strive for, but humans are animals and have inherent weakness and therefore will continue to make mistakes. To promote an idea of perfection is doing a great disservice to humans. It actually can make them feel horrible about themselves, as they can never live up to God's "heaven on earth" where everything is perfect. Humans are fallible. Living good-enough lives and doing one's best is a much more realistic and reasonable way to view the world as opposed to trying to obtain perfection which is unachievable.

The second premise (the community and social): religious systems are *not necessary* anymore for humans to be organized and thriving within a community/society. Spirituality does not need to include religion or a belief in a god. When we realize that we are being, or have been, manipulated by religion, we might feel very angry. However, habits and traditions die hard. We might just keep going to the same church/religion we grew up with. We might think that going to church and praying can help us when we find ourselves in a tough situation. Or, when we want a connection with a community, we might think that going to a church or finding solace in religion will comfort us. And it might very well do that in the short term, but in the long term, religions fail to deliver on many fronts (discussed later). Religion was institutionalized to purposefully target grief, depression, anxiety, failure, loneliness, and confusion in large social groups. Religion purposefully uses these human vulnerable states as opportunities for conversion to the faith. Our brains evolved to sometimes blur the lines between reality and other (this happens with chants, recitations, prayers, and hallucinogenic drugs). Religious systems take advantage of that brain trait[13]. More on this later on.

The third premise (the global level): the reason for many of the world's violent conflicts has to do with religions. They are flawed, extreme and punitive belief systems, and if we believe them, we are fooling ourselves. Country leaders are fooling

---

13   Turner, J.et al. *The Emergence and Evolution of Religion: By Means of Natural Selection*. Routledge. 2017.

themselves when they put religious/god-belief ahead of humanity as a whole.

You might say, what is the harm of believing in God if I get comfort and camaraderie with others at church? My response is that when the whole premise of getting together and praying is based on a lie (that is, a belief in God who will help us), it doesn't serve anyone well. Religious doctrines are mostly very black and white. And very authoritarian. This top-down and dogmatic approach can lead to judging others and identifying differences among peoples rather than focusing on their common humanity. Religious systems do not want us to think for ourselves. They survive and succeed by oppressing serious challenges to their authority. I would argue they have no authority, but that is another discussion altogether. However, getting together with the common aim of helping others is a very good thing. My suggestion is to take out the middleman (that is, religion/god) and just do good work (humanism).

> *"To believe something in the face of evidence and against reason—to believe something by faith—is ignoble, irresponsible, and ignorant, and merits the opposite of respect."*
> A. C. Grayling

> *"The unconsidered life is not worth living."*
> Socrates

"All great truths begin as blasphemies."
George Bernard Shaw

Our own belief system is carried out into the world. We could be more successful in increasing personal, community and world peace, and harmony and health of populations if we lost the middleman (religious systems and god-belief). Dealing in reality and facing life straight on, rather than in denial of facts, will lead to a happier more rewarding life, and by extrapolation, a better world. It's like direct selling—take out the middleman and get to the essence of the deal (and pay less—for example, tithing to churches). The deal I'm suggesting is looking at the reality of your own life and making the choices you need to improve in areas that need it. Later in the book, I recommend using qualified specialists (not quacks) if you need additional help in any area of your life. The other thing to remember is that religion is not a magic pill. It is not going to solve your problems—you are. No one but you can make the changes on the inside to take outside to the world. Do not delude yourself into thinking that a better life awaits you after death. (How can this idea continue to be peddled by religion?) Deal with the here and now, and make this your best life. Don't wait—time waits for no-one.

*"Forget Jesus. The stars died so that you could be here
today. Every atom in your body came from a star
that exploded."*

*"The purpose of education is not to validate
ignorance, but to overcome it."*

*"The real thing that physics tells us about the universe
is that big, rare events happen all the time—including
life—and that doesn't mean it's special."*

Lawrence Krauss

RELIGION VERSUS HUMANISM AND SKEPTICISM/ATHEISM

Humanism and Atheism are not new. Way back in the sixth
or fifth century BCE, the classical period (considered to be
between the eighth century BC to about the sixth century
AD), philosophical atheistic thought was expressed by many,
including Socrates, Euripedes, Aristophanes, Diagoras, and
Protagoras, and likely others. They questioned the mainstream
belief system of that time (polytheism = belief in many different gods). Throughout history, religion has tried to suppress
voices of reason. Religion, in general, has never been good
for intellectual advances. In fact, scientists and skeptics in the
past were often penalized severely (often by losing their lives
or livelihood or being exiled from their country) for challenging religious doctrine. Examples of this are Galileo (1564-1642)

who was tried by the Inquisition and put under house arrest, and then burned at the stake by the Catholic Church. Baruch Spinoza (1632-1677) had to flee Amsterdam and move to the Hague for challenging the authenticity of the Hebrew Bible. He never even said he didn't believe in God, he just questioned the church doctrines of the time. For this, he was expelled from his own Jewish community, including by his own family. The Catholic Church added his books to their "Index of Forbidden Books." His magnum opus *Ethics* is considered a masterpiece of philosophy. He moved thought forward for humankind, but paid a very high price for his questioning mind.

Advances in this world have most often been made by people willing to be outsiders from mainstream thought. Skeptics and freethinkers have often discovered ways that help humans expand their viewpoints and improve the quality of life for millions (for example, Thomas Edison, inventor of electricity delivery systems, among many other discoveries that changed the world for the better).

RELIGION AND THE MEDIEVAL ERA (476-1492 AD)

Some historians[14],[15],[16] have said that, had the intellectual movement not been suppressed by the Catholic Church, we would
never have had the Dark or Middle Ages. There have been
estimates that the human race might have had their scientific
discoveries benefiting the world a thousand years earlier, had
the Catholic Church not executed and punished anyone who
dared challenge their superstitious tenets. To this day, where
religion is strongest (for examples—Pakistan, Iran, Syria, Saudi
Arabia, Afghanistan), people are living somewhat like they did
in the Middle Ages. Outside of any emotional reaction to this,
one has to only look at the health indicators, to see these are not
healthy or happy societies. These are modern-day examples of
being stuck in the Dark Ages, where tribal and feudal warfare
was the norm.

Religion, a system of beliefs and rules, developed to *control and
monitor* people in larger groups[17]. It was also a way to transmit
knowledge through telling ancestral stories. When people
first lived in tribes, storytelling was the main way to pass

---

14 Hitchens, C. *God is Not Great: How Religion Poisons Everything*. Hachette
    Books. 2007.

15 Fieser, J. *Medieval Philosophy*. 2020. www.utm.edu.

16 www.plato.stanford.edu

17 Boyer, P. *Religion Explained. The human instincts that fashion gods,
    spirits and ancestors*. London. Vintage. 2002

information on to the young. Eventually from hunting and gathering tribes, where grooming each other was the social-bonding mechanism, the agricultural feudal system evolved. When cities began forming, there were too many people for monitoring by the group itself (anything over about 150 people and social monitoring is difficult). A more elaborate religious system evolved. When strangers found themselves living in close arrangements in the cities that were forming about a thousand years ago, religion began functioning as a major social monitor. Grooming each other didn't work anymore—as there were too many strangers for this intimate behaviour, and it would take too much time. The rules were clear—attend church weekly, get read the rules over and over, and if you broke any of the rules, know that you would burn in hell. The Church/priests had the most power of anyone. They were able to read; the masses were illiterate. Justice and legal systems were not in place, so religion held sway over people. The history of the Dark Ages is just that—very dark. The idea that there was an all-knowing god watching over everyone fulfilled the purposes of rules for everyone to follow, social bonding, and ritualized common behaviour.

Steven Pinker's book, *The Better Angels of Our Nature*, shows how violently and horribly humans treated each other. Punishments were severe and torture was common. Until the Reformation, this period was characterized by pretty miserable lives for most people. Life spans were short (it took luck to live into your thirties and forties; older age was the exception, not the rule) and life was extremely hard. The focus for people of this time period was simply survival—having enough food, clothing, and shelter to survive occupied most of their time. The hope for a better future or afterlife made life bearable for humans living in such difficult conditions (no running water, no electricity, no central heat). Just to gather firewood to keep the shelters warm enough and to cook food occupied a lot of their time. Not to mention the hard, physical drudgery of farm and agricultural work that people had to endure daily just to live. Sewage ran freely in towns and cities and infectious diseases spread rapidly. Influenza and other viruses killed thousands and thousands of people yearly, and there was always the threat of a new plague. If only the anti-vaccination people could be shown the horror of what is possible when vaccines are not available, they might change their minds.

RELIGION AS A MONEY-MAKING BUSINESS,[18,19,] A CULT[20] AND MIND MANIPULATOR[21]

Another reason that religion is so entrenched and has so much to lose is that churches are essentially money-making businesses. In reality, the only difference between a religion and a cult is how much they own, and their membership numbers. If one looks up the definition of cult in the Oxford dictionary, it says "a religious belief system." The Catholic Church owns massive amounts of land, art, and buildings. They have a lot to lose. This is the best example of religion owning wealth, but most churches are the same. They have to pay for the buildings, the priests/preachers, and all the programs they run. They cling to their wealth, power, and ability to manipulate and control peoples' emotions. It's much harder these days to hide the corruption and abuses due to social media. No longer can the religions/cults hide what has really been going on since they started.

---

18 Grim, B. *Religion may be bigger business than we thought. Here's why.* WEF Annual Meeting. 2017.

19 Rienzi, M.L. *God and the Profits: Is there Religious Liberty for Money-Makers?* The Catholic University of America, Columbus School of Law Faculty. Scholarly Articles. 2013

20 Rodia, T. Is it a cult, or a new religious movement? University of Pennsylvania. Religious Studies. 2019.

21 Azarian, B. PhD. *How Religious Fundamentalism Hijacks the Brain.* Psychology Today. October, 2018.

The main place that religion seems to find new followers is in developing and dysfunctional countries where people may not have access to education or progress. Especially when people are poor, they need hope. Religion gives them that, however it fails to deliver most of what it promises (salvation, life after death)—as these are not measurable and are extremely unlikely. The other group of individuals that have no choice in the matter is children. When children are brought up within a religious cult, they usually conform and believe just as their parents do. Sometimes when they are older and really think about the myths that have been fed to them as truths, they figure it out. However, because the pull of magical and wishful thinking is very strong, many cannot resist it.

All humans, however, remain susceptible to the lies and promises that religions offer, but cannot deliver on. There are a few isolated cults/religious groups that maintain followers by staying separate from mainstream societies on purpose (often in compounds), and controlling the information available to members (Rajneeshees, the People's Temple, Hare Krishna, the Moonies—the Unification Church, Scientology as some examples). But *all religions are cults*—it's just the size of the cult that determines whether it is called a cult or a religion.

Mainstream religions have just been legitimized by a larger number of people, but they are still cults. When we think of cults, we think they are full of weird or bizarre rituals, prayers/incantations. But how is this any different than those rituals and processes within the Catholic Church? Take, for example, the concept of *reincarnation* (Jesus rising to Heaven from being dead) and *transubstantiation* (in the Catholic Church the wafer and wine are supposed to literally be the body and blood of Christ)—this is legitimized completely by Catholics. If we stop to think about this concept—does it not seem absurd? Rituals, chanting/prayers, and symbols seem to mesmerize people into complacency and comfort. The Jews have "shuckling" – swaying back and forth while praying. The Muslims have bowing, hand gestures, prostration and chanting prayers. The Christians have many similar rituals and gestures.

Religion and church leaders purposefully engage followers in magical-thinking—miracles can happen—these cut right to the *primitive amygdala* or *feeling-brain* emotions of love, fear, shame, and anger. Note the similarity between sports teams or political rallies where people chant slogans and repeat the same words over and over—very much like churches who have the congregation do the same. Note the definition of demagogue is a "a leader or agitator who wins support by appealing to people's *feelings, emotions* and prejudices rather than appealing to logic." Does this not describe most priests/pastors/rabbis when talking about Bible stories?

This chanting/praying or reciting creeds employs the limbic (midbrain) system, which can lead to feelings of oneness with the group. This is a very powerful way to engage people in losing themselves—meaning that the higher-level thinking is suppressed while a person repeats a creed or a slogan or prays with others, and chanting the same words. A lot of people come out of these chanting/prayer sessions feeling calmed. In this way, even though the words might make very little sense, people are temporarily comforted. Once you realize this, you might feel very manipulated. *It is manipulation*, and that is one of the main reasons to be appalled by how religion uses people's vulnerability to these types of processes/behaviors (the prayers, the chanting, the readings together, all at once).

RELIGION, CULTURE AND POWER[22]

According to anthropologist Clifford Geertz's book on religion, *The Interpretation of Cultures* (1973), humans cannot live outside of culture. He defines religion as: (1) A system of symbols which acts to (2) Establish powerful, pervasive, and long-lasting moods in people by (3) Formulating conceptions of a general order of existence and (4) Clothing those conceptions in such an *aura of factuality* that (5) The moods and motivations *seem* uniquely realistic. In other words, religions fool

---

22   Havea, J.(editor). *Religion and Power*. Rowman and Littlefield. Lexington Books. Fortress Academic. ISBN 9781978703568. 2020.

followers into believing in many strange and weird things (such as transubstantiation and reincarnation).

Religions purposefully deceive us, for cultural reasons. A big concept inherent within the structure of religion is power. This is the power to *control* people and to give them a group identity. The problem with this is the inherent issue of *separateness* or *specialness* of the identified group. Christians, Muslims, and Jews can believe they are special or better than other groups because they have figured out the true way of being. The narrative that the Jews have always had is that they are God's Chosen People. Each religion has at its core, the idea that they are the right and true group. This is tragically flawed in relation to current world affairs. Maintaining separateness does nothing to make other groups feel included or welcome. It's a real problem for peace in the world when different religious groups refuse to change their ways based on their faith and the interpretation of their holy books. *No one group is special.* They really are just about the same as other groups. We've enabled this idea of specialness in our societies by continuing to allow special interest groups to flourish. Human rights are extremely important, but we need to get away from the separateness-thinking that has encouraged many groups to believe that they deserve *preferential* treatment over another group. We need to have an inclusive mind-set rather than an exclusive mind-set. We need to see each person as simply human and not identify them with a religious group.

The need for community and emotional connection is so strong that some people leave common sense behind. The rituals, symbols, and readings/scriptures give a group a common purpose and structure. Power, identity, and ritual are such strong human needs that people will overlook the real problems within the system in order for it to continue functioning. We need to use higher-level reasoning to move away from the traditional, outdated religions and toward modern secular groups (with oversight, democratic representatives, and checks and balances), that can offer the same meaning, purpose, and identity to fulfill those basic human needs.

> *"If God did not exist, then we would have to invent him."*
> Voltaire

And that is exactly what humans have done. Humans invented god and religious systems. They are simply constructs created by humans to comfort themselves and tell stories from the past (which may or may not be relevant to current times).

Nowadays, (in the twenty-first century), neither is beneficial nor necessary. We have better ways of comforting ourselves and our loved ones (examples: meditation, volunteering, humanist group work). We also can be spiritual without religion.

RELIGION VERSUS SCIENTIFIC EVIDENCE[23]

Religion has never been able to deliver what it promises—there is no proof of an afterlife and we don't see the magic and miracles happen (as they apparently did in the holy books)—but we see science changing the world for the better.

Victor Stenger, eminent American physicist, said it best: "Science flies you to the moon; Religion flies you into buildings."

(I wrote this just after the eighteenth anniversary of the New York City twin towers' complete destruction by terrorists; Sept 11, 2001).

There is also the problem of unanswered prayers, and the plain facts that the Christian God is certainly not benevolent, does not have a plan, and is not all-knowing. There are no good studies showing prayer makes any difference on outcomes, although many people will gladly offer *testimonials* stating they are convinced that their prayers were answered. I'd like to know how many prayers remain unanswered. There is the problem of continued suffering for many people. Despite praying, people continue to get cancer and other diseases. Why would a benevolent god wish this on anyone? When a child gets cancer, it is hard to see how that would fit into God's plan. What

---

23   Coyne, J. *Faith vs. Fact. Why Science and Religion are Incompatible.* Viking Press. 2015.

is God's plan anyway? Scientists such as Stenger, Dawkins, and Hawking have answered this by saying essentially, what we see in our world is exactly what would be expected from no plan, no designer, and no god.

> *"The universe we observe has precisely the properties we should expect if there is, at bottom, no design, no purpose, no evil, no good, nothing but blind pitiless indifference. Biology is the study of complicated things that have the appearance of having been designed with purpose."*
> Richard Dawkins

> *"We are the product of quantum fluctuations in the very early universe."*
> *"We are just an advanced breed of monkeys on a minor planet of a very average star. But we can understand the universe. That makes us something very special."*
> Steven Hawking

One of saddest situations I saw in my health care career, was when people turned to God after they had been diagnosed with a disease/cancer of some sort. It's very understandable why one might choose to do this. At this point, the person and their family are likely desperate to try anything that might help them recover or gain more time to live. In churches, there will often be group prayers and the members of the church are certainly well intentioned by praying for the sick and needy. Everyone involved is comforted temporarily and so everyone *feels* better. It is the ultimate consolation story to be told you actually never die—you just go to Heaven. In this way of thinking, for many people, death is not final, and they are comforted by this thought. This sense of calm and decreased anxiety could be equally achieved by meditation or supportive group therapy/social club membership. Religion is not necessary, and again, it is incorrect to believe that there is a god who has any influence whatsoever on health outcomes. And ultimately, one must ask oneself, why would God give me cancer in the first place if he's so benevolent, all-knowing, and has a plan? Getting cancer or a disease just doesn't seem to fit into any good plan.

As to the studies indicating church attenders experience lower levels of depression and anxiety, the results are to be expected. These types of results could be similarly obtained by volunteering, humanism work, or any type of *regular positive engagement* with a group of people—family/friends/work colleagues. It is *social isolation* that tends to increase depression and anxiety; there are many positive ways to address this other than going to church.

RELIGION AND EDUCATION[24,25]

History matters. Until the last few hundred years, we saw education available only to a select few (priests, ministers, aristocrats/nobility), but as the world has become more literate and people travel and see more, religious doctrine can and should be questioned increasingly by everyone. Most of us don't take a lot of time to question the religious institutions that surround us. Perhaps we inherited a religion from our family, our culture, or our country. Now that we have so much more information available to us, we must critically examine these systems. We must demand of our elected officials that public funds should not support any institutions where there is no outside oversight, checks and balances, and democratically elected officials. In other words, religion has no place whatsoever in the public sphere. And we must educate the youth about history and reality today.

During the Reformation (c. 1517-1600), when the Catholic Church was strongly challenged by Protestants, the basic Christian faith remained. Protestants were on the right track by questioning papal authority. Some of the key leaders were Martin Luther and John Calvin. Slowly, the powers of the Catholic Church decreased. The sale of indulgences—basically

---

24   Pew Research Center. Religious Landscape Study, 2014.

25   Zuckerman, P. *Why Education Corrodes Religious Faith*. *The Secular Life*. Psychology Today. 2014.

buying your way into Heaven—was identified as wrong by Luther, and eventually he was excommunicated (kicked out of the Catholic Church). Churches were very profitable as a business model, and the priests lived very well indeed. Luther also rejected the Catholic Church's doctrine of transubstantiation. Semantics was key in separating different factions of Christianity. Today, we see, and have seen, many iterations and interpretations of created religious rules. One of the most interesting was the creation of the Anglican Church in England by King Henry VIII (1491—1547) because the pope would not give him a divorce. So, he rejected the pope's authority and the Catholic Church and made up his own Church. To this day, it is known as the Church of England or the Anglican Church.

Schools must do a better job of teaching world history, not just local or national history. In Canada, for example, very little time is spent teaching about how world history led to our current systems of education and government. For example, most children or young adults in Canada (or adults for that matter) do not understand how important the Reformation, Renaissance, and French Revolution were. If you tried to have a discussion with most people about the changes that the Reformation, Renaissance, and French Revolution brought, you'd likely get a very blank stare. It's necessary to repeat these lessons that are so important, as most of us readily forget what we are taught. We cannot afford to take those historical changes lightly; the fact that we do have separation of church and state is hugely important. Without continual reminders of these hard-won changes, we risk falling backwards towards demagoguery and authoritarianism (which is how, generally, religious leaders operate). To see and hear politicians speak about God is not a good thing—wars and revolutions happened so that religion would not dominate our government, legal, and education systems. One of the most bizarre behaviours I've witnessed recently is that a certain world leader is publicly showing off his "supportive spiritual team." This is alarmingly regressive—the monarchs in the past used to do this, and it should stay in the past. The slow creeping-in of spiritual leaders and religion into mainstream politics is worrisome.

RELIGION & HEALTH MEASURES[26], CRITICAL ANALYSIS[27] AND THE SCIENTIFIC METHOD[28]

With regard to health measures, referencing the UN's World Happiness Report (2018, 150 countries compared), The World Values Survey (2016, almost 100 countries compared), and the Human Development Index (2018 report), is that overall, the more secular countries tend to have better health, wealth, and

---

26   Paul, G. Successful Societies Scale & WIN-Gallop International Global Index of Religiosity and Atheism. 2012.

27   What is Critical Analysis? www.bradford.ac.uk, workshops.

28   Scientific Method. Plato.stanford.edu & www.britannica.com

well-being indicators than religious countries. For example, Finland, Denmark, Norway, and Sweden rank very high on happiness levels as well as other health indicators, such as long life, gender parity, and higher levels of education obtained across their population. Happier countries also tend to rate higher in areas of life social support, freedom to make life choices, and lowest levels of government corruption. Some countries such as Mexico have, as a whole, very content and happy populations, however, they have major corruption within their legal/justice systems, so they do not rank highly in happiness indices overall. They are also lacking in access to good education and health care *across their whole population*, so they fall lower overall in the rankings.

In general, the more functional and secular a country, the healthier and happier are the people within it. The trend is clear as far as what is required to have a thriving, healthy, and happy country. Although correlation is not causation, there is definitely a strong trend that when countries develop and progress (become more functional), religiosity decreases. The most successful countries also have the best public health systems emphasizing education, vaccination, and birth control as well as generous maternity and paternity-leave options. They have longer life expectancies, lower obesity levels, higher rates of breastfeeding for longer durations and infant and maternal mortality rates are very low[29].

Circa 2020, we live in an age of continual disruption, change, fake news, real news, and everything in between (and actually, it has always been thus)! Humans, in general, love information and gossip, and we base decision-making on the sum of all the information that our brains process. But how can we know what is true and valid and what is not? With multitudes of information hitting us daily (if not by the minute or hour), with our phones (social media such as Facebook, Instagram, Twitter), our televisions, and print media (magazines, newspapers) we all have to become more competent in critical analysis. By this, I mean that in schools we need to start teaching these skills to younger children—that is, when the imaginary world of children naturally dissipates around ages ten to twelve, we need to teach them to replace that magical-thinking, miracles-can-happen, imaginary-beings-exist mentality of fairy tales, with critical thinking. This generally happens naturally when children figure out on their own that Santa Claus is not real. The main fairy tale that seems to persist within some people is that their imaginary God exists.

Interesting to note, most god believers were infected with the myth/superstition of a God existing when they were very

---

29   OECD Health Statistics, 2017.

young. When one looks at the numbers, it is much rarer to see people come to God later in life because their frontal lobe and reasoning abilities have developed and matured over time. They generally can see the God myth as just that—another big fairy tale. It is not unheard of (for example, "Born Again Christians") but certainly most of the god believers have been infected with the superstitious virus from birth, which really is unfair, because it was not their choice. Brain injury or disease can also cause some to experience a religious experience or revelation due to altering the structure of the brain. Psychoactive drugs such as mescaline, psilocybin, and LSD can also alter the brain's information processing, and it is well established in medical literature that revelations and religious/spiritual experiences are common under the influence of these drugs[30].

This critical analysis topic is covered in some of the school curriculums, but it needs to become of utmost importance. Young children and teenagers are especially gullible and susceptible to lies/bad information, etc. This god myth is perpetuated by the huge amounts of garbage-type information that is all over the place. With free speech also comes the problem of much inaccurate information, and perhaps outright lies. It is also unfortunate that many celebrities like to promote their own

---

30   Pollan, Michael. *What the New Science of Psychedelics Teaches Us About Consciousness, Addiction, Depression and Transcendence.*   Penguin Press. 2018.

versions of religious/mystical/superstitious belief systems. And many people, with our gullible brains, fall for it left, right, and centre. Therefore, it is crucial that people learn how to analyze what is real and true and what is not…and what is really of no importance at all.

What is utterly incredible and seems the most hypocritical and reprehensible of all the behaviours I have witnessed, is the ability of otherwise very intelligent, sane people who allow faith a complete pass from challenge/evaluation/scrutiny. I have heard medical doctors, lawyers, engineers and other highly educated people, discuss their religious beliefs. They are reasonable in their general lives and demand fact-based evidence for all other areas of their lives (such as health, government, or education). But they seem completely unaware of this blind spot. I will speak further about this cognitive dissonance, but I think it is worth repeating here as an example of willful denial of strong scientific evidence that refutes faith/biblical claims. For example, the bible states that God created the earth. The question of how the universe came into existence is called the *first cause argument*[31]. It suggests everything is caused by something else, therefore someone or something must have created the earth. But this is NOT true. Because we have repeated evidence of the Big Bang explosion about 13.7 billion years ago, we

---

31   BBC.co.uk Religious Studies. An Introduction to the Philosophy of Religion. GCSE CCEA. 2020.

know how the earth was created. It was not created by a God. If a God created the earth by the Big Bang, then who created God? This is a non-ending rhetorical question that can never be adequately explained. The Big Bang created our universe. And we know there are multi-verses. The idea that some supernatural being is overseeing and creating and managing these multiple universes is *simply not believable*. So when people claim they have "a personal relationship with God or Jesus Christ"—are we meant to believe they have an imaginary friend called Jesus Christ or God? A professional's credibility is questionable when they exhibit this cognitive distortion problem.

God believers might say that non-believers have faith in science. But that is like comparing apples and oranges. Science can be proven *with evidence*. The word faith itself asks one to suspend reason, logic, and sense, and to believe with no evidence at all. For example, the evidence is overwhelming that there is no god, yet some people in *this one area of their lives*, continue to ignore the science, and *choose* ignorance. As mentioned before, our best scientists have shown proofs of evolution and the Big Bang. However, many people seem perfectly ok with this one area not to be challenged—you are allowed to have your faith. You are allowed to have imaginary friends. Indeed, the current leader of the USA has an imaginary friend. And indeed, it is protected by constitutional right. However, in all other areas of life, we would never accept using faith as an appropriate information source versus evidence and science-based proofs.

Judging is not the intent in this book, but I will say that I find many religious believers very lacking in this area—a lot of people will overlook this personal blind spot very readily, while at the same time, calling out leaders and community members for their lack in some other character trait (for example, dishonesty with constituents regarding toxin levels in water). It's very hypocritical for religious people to criticize government, education, or health, when they themselves will not be challenged on their faith. This is cognitively dissonant—dishonesty with themselves, showing a major inconsistency in how that person thinks; that is, irrationally and not critically.

> *"Faith can be very dangerous, and deliberately to implant it into the vulnerable mind of a child is a grievous wrong."*
> *"Faith is the great cop-out, the great excuse to evade the need to think and evaluate evidence. Faith is the belief in spite of, even perhaps because of, the lack of evidence."*
> Richard Dawkins

"Religion provides the only story that is fundamentally consoling in the face of the worst possible experiences—the death of a parent, for instance. In fact, many religions take away the problem entirely, because their adherents believe that they're going to be reunited with everyone they love, and death is an illusion."
Sam Harris

"One cannot really argue with a mathematical theorem."
Stephen Hawking

This is where science/scientific method comes in. The source of the information must be determined. Is this a reputable source? Who has written the information and what are their qualifications and training? Are they a layperson or a trained specialist? People study for many, many years to become a specialist with recognized letters behind their name (M.D., PhD, PEng etc). Would I listen to them or to an illiterate charismatic leader (Jesus for example) regarding the recommendations for living a better life? Would I go to a medical doctor or a "faith healer" to help cure my cancer? It is your choice, but the most reasonable, logical and best choice would be to go to a medical doctor for help.

To be considered good evidence or factual, an experiment must be repeatable, and results must come out the same time after time. There are different types of experiments or studies, and a trained person knows how to assess the validity of the study. For example, an *anecdotal* study, where a few people say that a certain pill helps them lose weight, (these are often called "*testimonials*"), is not very useful in terms of validity. This means, we cannot use the testimonial results to apply to everybody in that population. Another common example of anecdotal/testimonial is when people claim to have had an out-of-body or near-death experience. It is well established that when the brain undergoes a severe stress such as lack of oxygen, or the body has been in a very prolonged fasting state(as Jesus was with his 40 days and nights in the desert) or is under the influence of psychoactive drugs, the brain processing can result in revelations/prophecies/insights. For example, epileptics have higher incidences of these after a brain seizure. People who have ingested psilocybin (magic mushrooms), mescaline, or LSD may undergo similar experiences. These insights/revelations/prophecies can generally be explained biologically.

Also praying—how many prayers go unanswered? Has anybody ever done that study? I would wager that the number of unanswered prayers far outweighs the number of answered prayers. As just one example, a research study looking at whether intercessory prayer had any effect on cardiovascular disease progression showed that praying had *no significant effect* on medical outcomes after hospitalizations in a coronary care unit.[32]

In contrast, if there are *multiple* studies with many, many, people (a meta-analysis), and with a randomized, control-blind design, or a surveillance or longitudinal type study that follows many thousands of people over generations, the results will carry far more weight, in the sense that results can be extrapolated to represent the population at large. This is very simplistic, however; there are strict rules that need to be followed to have results that mean anything. Scientists welcome challenge—this is how progress and knowledge increase. This is why they are encouraged to publish their work and make it widely available.

Peer review is another check on study design and methodology. With peer review, weaknesses and strengths are identified, and results assessed in light of these factors. In science, there is great competition, as well as collaboration. With a competitive, knowledge-driven and knowledge-seeking system, innovation and invention thrives. Whether your results come from Japan, Germany, or Canada, science is science. It can be proven or disproven. Science doesn't recognize a race/religion/creed, it only looks at evidence and proofs. Science doesn't care where you are

32   J.M. Aviles et al.   *Intercessory Prayer and Cardiovascular Disease Progression in a Coronary Care Unit Population: A Randomized Control Trial*.   Mayo Clinic Proc. Dec. 2001.

from, it only wants answers. It's an equal playing field, based on everyone following the same scientific processes. That is why you can read a study from Turkey and still use the results in the USA, if it is a valid study. Religion is the opposite. It doesn't like to be questioned or challenged (mostly because there are no good answers they can provide). It is not open to challenge as it purports to already know all the answers of the universe, with no evidence or proof. And this is why religion is regressive (going backwards), not just neutral.

Note: I used as my references in this book, people who are the best in their field—namely scientists and specialists of many types, who work at some of the best universities in the world (see references). This book is not at all about anything New Age, magic pills, or unproven theories. It really is an attempt to consolidate the best evidence from different areas, such as population health, physics, biology, chemistry, psychology, sociology, anthropology and some philosophy.

Change is good! It's the only way to improve and progress. I don't just mean technologies, medicine, and wealth. It would also include improvements in efficiencies, lifestyles, and global collaborations. Challenging the status quo is important. Many times, as seen historically and presently, there are improvements made in technology, education, etc., that can optimize areas of human lives. Look at vaccines, birth control, education. From the micro-level (individual) to the macro-level (population), removing religion is a very positive health idea. Why? Because without religion to divide us or confuse us with faulty beliefs, that is, delude us, we can focus on making real changes, right here, right now.

RELIGION AND SCIENCE AS INCOMPATIBLE NOTIONS[33,34] (COGNITIVE DISSONANCE)

The essence of this book is that science and religion are *incompatible*—science demands evidence and proof, and religion asks us to suspend these and believe in something unreal, unproven, and existing only in our imaginations. Religions, like infectious diseases, have been so infective within cultures that they can make us immune to seeing or hearing about the real truth of our world (that is, the result of being infected by religion is gaining a mental blind spot). The vector of transmission, like a disease, is both vertically (up and down through families) and horizontally—peer pressure or interactions with communities and social groups. Religions have been so effective because they work on our most primitive brain functions—fear, guilt, shame, and worry. Fear of possibly missing out on getting to

---

33   Coyne, J. *Faith vs Fact. Why Science and Religion are Incompatible.* Viking Press. 2015.

34   Bardon, A. *Coronavirus Responses Highlight How Humans Have Evolved to Dismiss Facts That Don't Fit Their Worldview. Science denialism is not just a simple matter of logic or ignorance.* The Conversation. June 26, 2020.

a (non-existent) Heaven, and shame, guilt, and worry for not fitting into the community that has been infected by the belief system. Social contagion—because others are doing it, we must too! This can be very dangerous. It's much easier to go along with the groupthink/herd mentality/emotional side than pause, think about facts, and realize you can't go along with the groupthink because they are wrong. Religion is like the magic pill way of thinking—sounds great, promises amazing results, but delivers zero. Religion does not want you to think for yourself, but just to follow the rules, follow what you are told, and everything will be just fine. Not true.

RELIGION (CREATIONISM AND INTELLIGENT DESIGN) VS SCIENCE

Please see the writings of Richard Dawkins, Sam Harris, Daniel Dennett, Steven Hawking, Victor Stenger, Lawrence Krauss, and many more eminent scientists, for full explanations of lack of scientific proofs for God and the reasoning behind these assertions. Charles Darwin, one of the fathers of the theory of evolution, has been proven correct time and time again. A more contemporary scientist, Dr. Jerry Coyne (American biologist, evolutionary geneticist, University of Chicago), has provided clear evidence that conclusively shows there can be no intelligent design, or any other newfangled creationist idea. There are evolutionary proofs provided by: transitional fossils, embryology, molecular biology, the presence of vestigial organs and biogeography (a common African ancestor for all humankind—meaning that really there is no race; we're all of the human race).

Recently, creationists have tried to defend the idea of intelligent design based on the ability of humans to have abstract thought and language. This is utter nonsense, as from an evolutionary perspective; the fossil record indicates the development of hand tools from simple rocks, which indicates abstract thinking—that is the ability to create a slightly more evolved tool from a chunk of rock. With respect to language, there are cognitive psychologists (Steven Pinker for example) who have offered very convincing evidence of evolution from simple sound or language chunks to higher-level language development. The intelligent-design believers are grasping at straws. As said before by many eminent scientists (Hawking, Stenger, Feynman, Dawkins), our world as it currently exists, reflects exactly what one would expect from *no design, no creator, and no god*.

RELIGION AND VIOLENCE[35]

So much of human strife (violent conflicts and wars) and suffering (diseases, mental anguish) is caused by deluding ourselves. Facing reality head-on can help with our own health and the health

---

35   Jerryson, M. et al. (editors). *The Oxford Handbook of Religion and Violence*. 2013.

of our communities, cities, countries, and world. When we start with ourselves (our health, wealth, and wellness) we can then look outward and use the same evidence-based facts to guide our decision making for our communities, cities, states, and countries.

Gapminder.org and Steven Pinker's books (*Enlightenment Now* and *The Better Angel of Our Natures*) show the numbers regarding the overall declines in world violence as secularism has increased. Just a quick review of history shows the Holocaust (Hitler was supposedly a good Catholic, and Germans were mostly Christian), the Inquisition, the Witch Trials, the Crusades, the corruption and sexual abuses within (not only) the Catholic Church, and all the other religious wars to get an idea of the damage done by religion. Back in the Ancient and Middle Ages, horrendous numbers of people were killed with frequent wars among different tribes. Today, we continue to see conflicts in the world based on religious persecutions (examples, the Rohingya in Myanmar, the Yazidis in Iraq and Syria, the Uyghurs in China). In the name of religion, different factions continue to fight and kill each other.

Many people will mention the good done by religious groups. I don't deny that many good and charitable works have been carried out in the name of religion. However, very frequently, there is a condition that the recipients of the charity convert to that religion (especially true with Christians). And consequently, when identifying as a certain religion (for example,

"I'm a Christian"), a possible reason for division among people is introduced even though that is not the intention. It is a very damaging possible side-effect with possibly devasting consequences (for example, war). We only have to look at the present-day Middle East to see how damaging religious beliefs continue to fuel ongoing devastation, violence, and aggression there. Good charitable work can and should be done without religion. Doctors Without Borders is a wonderful example.

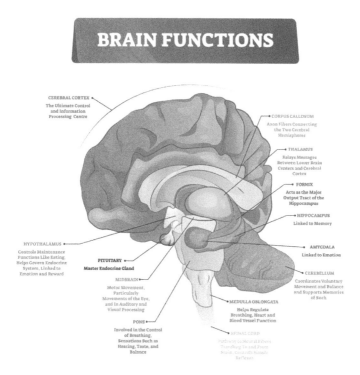

BRAIN FUNCTIONS

CEREBRAL CORTEX
The Ultimate Control and Information Processing Centre

CORPUS CALLOSUM
Axon Fibers Connecting the Two Cerebral Hemispheres

THALAMUS
Relays Messages Between Lower Brain Centers and Cerebral Cortex

FORNIX
Acts as the Major Output Tract of the Hippocampus

HIPPOCAMPUS
Linked to Memory

HYPOTHALAMUS
Controls Maintenance Functions Like Eating, Helps Govern Endocrine System, Linked to Emotion and Reward

PITUITARY
Master Endocrine Gland

MIDBRAIN
Motor Movement, Particularly Movements of the Eye, and In Auditory and Visual Processing

AMYGDALA
Linked to Emotion

CEREBELLUM
Coordinates Voluntary Movement and Balance and Supports Memories of Such

MEDULLA OBLONGATA
Helps Regulate Breathing, Heart and Blood Vessel Function

PONS
Involved in the Control of Breathing, Sensations Such as Hearing, Taste, and Balance

SPINAL CORD
Pathway to Neural Fibers Traveling To and From Brain, Controls Simple Reflexes

RELIGION, NEUROBIOLOGY, AND PSYCHOLOGY (LOCUS OF CONTROL, PERSONALITY TRAITS)[36,37]

It's important to emphasize that it's our *neuro-biological evolution* that has led humans to this place and given us our history of war and violence—by making illogical choices based in fear and shame (using the lower level or primitive part of our brain) and not using the higher-level executive functions of the pre-frontal lobe and neo-cortex. Using higher level thinking, we can make better, that is, reasonable, decisions. Moving away from religion (lower, more primitive thinking), and using humanism (higher level thinking) is a way forward. Just because we can use religion in our lives, doesn't mean it's right or good to use religion in our lives anymore. We have so much more knowledge available to us now that supports transitioning away from religion. It is like the next step in our evolution as a species—a more evolved way (rational/thinking brain) than being stuck in the primitive fear and shame that religion teaches. I do recognize that this will never happen completely because as this book shows, humans remain very vulnerable to emotionally triggering fairy tales, superstition, myths, and mysticism. But

---

36 Boyer, P. *Religion Explained: The Evolutionary Origins of Religious Thought*. Basic Books, 2001.

37 Barrett, J.L. *Why Would Anyone Believe in God?* Rowman and Littlefield. 2004.

if the numbers of rational people increase, it will do a lot for humankind in terms of increasing world functionality.

Humans have three general areas in the brain—lower, mid-brain, and frontal cortex. Religious beliefs and doctrines play into our most basic emotions—fear, shame, guilt, and worry. These emotions are processed in the more primitive region where there is no higher reasoning (no executive function). This is where involuntary reactions take place—for example, breathing and the fight-or-flight reflex. We don't think about these things, our bodies just do them automatically. For reasoning and higher-level thinking, another part of the brain called the pre-frontal cortex is used. Since we know this and are aware of this, we should recognize it for what it is—religions prey (pun intended) on the vulnerable, emotional, and lower level (primitive) functioning of our brains. This helps explain why people turn to religion when they experience trouble or want comfort. With praying and reciting, the lower level and midbrain (limbic system) are engaged to comfort us—repeating the same prayers, reciting incantations, and being in a common group help comfort and allay distress and anxiety.

In fact, the sense of self is suppressed by the chanting—and can result in the feeling of oneness with the group/congregation. The midbrain (limbic area) acts as a sensory-input modulator. With the prayers, chants, and recitations, the midbrain is soothed, and emotions dampened. What is wrong with this? Well, first off, people are praying to something that doesn't exist—in other words they are actively deluding themselves. Much like a band-aid/temporary solution, church-going and praying might help in the short term, but for the long term can offer zero. If a person gets into the habit of self-delusion, it can really cause issues. It can lead a person to not take responsibility for their life in other areas. If one believes "it's in God's hands," this belief takes away power and control over one's own life (known as agency = I have control over my life)[38]. What this means is that rather than an internal locus of control (I am in control of my choices, I am responsible, I am accountable), an external locus of control is used (it's in God's hands, I have no power to choose, there's nothing I can do about it). On a mass scale, we can see whole nations using this approach—this is what our God demands we do. This is from our holy book that tells us to protect our land and our tribe. That's the kind of mentality that starts wars!

As a registered dietitian for many years in hospitals and public health clinics, I saw this over and over again. Many people blame something outside of themselves for their health issues. This is understandable but not helpful for improving their health

---

38   Cirhinlioglu, F.G. & Ozdekmenli-Demir, G. *Religious Orientation and its relation to Locus of Control and Depression.* Archive for the Psychology of Religion, 34, 341-62. March 2018.

condition. It must be noted here that *most* humans are predisposed to developing chronic health problems (such as heart disease, high blood pressure, obesity and type 2 diabetes) due to our evolution to store fat (energy). Although genetics plays a small role, many lifestyle changes can help prevent, control and manage these diseases. It takes a lot of hard work and discipline to stay fit and eat healthfully. But rather than accepting and acting on this, many people simply say there is nothing they can do about their health. Taking away internal locus of control is not a good thing. It's giving up personal responsibility. There is actually a religious saying to go along with this idea—God helps those who help themselves—recognizing that there is much we can and should do to take charge of our own health based on the reality of the here and now, and not on the promise of something outside of us having power over us (because let's face it, God isn't able to help you with your health; you are). Putting oneself in the role of victim is the opposite of being responsible for all areas in one's life.

Certainly, there are many things we have no control over, but with regard to preventable chronic diseases such as type 2 diabetes, heart disease, and high blood pressure, there are many personal lifestyle choices that can influence the disease progression. If we develop a health condition/disease, it is still better to focus on the medical/science-based help along with meditation, mindfulness-relaxation, and group therapy (which achieve similar comforting outcomes, without the lie of a God being involved) as opposed to praying to a non-existent God. Spiritual, non-religious practices such as meditation, yoga, and mindfulness, have been shown to decrease anxiety and stress levels and help with health outcomes[39]. Social support is extremely important, but this can be obtained outside of any religious system.

Why is it even important to worry about the prevention of these long-term chronic diseases? These are precisely the diseases that *cost* every health system the most in terms of money, loss of productivity, and opportunity costs. In other words, they drain the health system dry of funds because they are relentlessly insidious and continue for long periods of time before death arrives. Obviously, with aging comes an increase of incidence and prevalence of diseases, but if we can push the age of disease development back as much as possible, it is in all societies' best interests. The goal would be to increase the number of years people are healthy and not needing the health system.

Personality traits also strongly influence a person's likeliness to follow a religious system. Out of five main personality traits (levels of: agreeableness, openness, extraversion, conscientiousness, neuroticism), highly extraverted, agreeable and

---

39 Kabat-Zinn, J. *Mindfulness Meditation for Everyday Life.* Sound Horizons. 1994.

highly conscientious traits are highly correlated to religiosity[40]. Growing up in a religious household also is highly influential in whether or not a person becomes religious. People that grow up in a non-religious family but exhibit these same traits are more likely to become secular humanitarians. Perhaps both believers and nonbelievers are adaptive to society, providing checks and balances amongst individuals. Religiosity is likely to be more adaptive in *dysfunctional societies* (lower democracy, lower social security, lower income equality, higher disease rates, higher mortality, suicide, poverty and unemployment). Atheism is perhaps more useful in successful (better functioning) societies[41].

I recognize that reason will not work for everyone—many people are too invested in their positions. It seems that some people see it as defeat when they admit error, as if being reasonable and logical versus spiritual and emotional was some sort of competition. It is not a competition. There is a time and place for emotion. But for best decision making, in the long term, using reason and science are much better. Sometimes we all must admit our errors—in thinking, in choices we've made, etc. And science welcomes correction. Science asks that we try to prove it wrong. Science is always up for debate. Religion has

40   Khoynezhad, G., Rajaei, A. & Sarvarazemy, A. Basic Religious Beliefs and Personality Traits. Iranian Journal of Psychiatry. Spring; 7(2): 82-86. 2012.

41   Hewer, M. *The Roots of Religion. Association for Psychological Science.* August 31, 2016.

never asked that. The doctrines do not want you thinking for yourself. And that is a problem. Part of the human condition is to make mistakes. Every human makes mistakes, and owning up to these mistakes is liberating because we can learn from the mistakes and move forward (and hopefully not repeat them). Humanism principles encourage science and evidence to base decisions on.

Unfortunately, oftentimes the most vulnerable people are most susceptible to the lure of religion's false promises. This is why there is a problem with faith-based charities. For example, if a faith-based charity offers homeless people shelter, food, and clothing, they are almost guaranteed to offer prayers and inclusion in the church community. While it seems harmless, in fact it is reproachable, because the church is basically preying (pun intended) on the needy to get followers. When someone offers a hungry homeless person a meal and a prayer, boom—come join the creed. This could be likened to offering a person in pain some opioids on an ongoing basis. Sure, the intention is to decrease suffering, but the end result is addiction and self-delusion. The suffering person is soothed in the short term, and in the long term—major issues—in that they cannot get off the drug. In fact, this was Jesus' message to the poor, needy, outcast, and hopeless. Come join my cult, and you will be soothed and saved. The people who converted to Christianity were generally the down and outers—outcasts, beggars, and slaves—people who were desperate and on the sidelines of society. These people had pretty miserable lives, so the message Jesus was promoting was fit for the time and extremely enticing. When life was very harsh and brutal, it made a lot of sense to follow this new cult. The problem is the promises of salvation and Heaven are lies. Only a person can save themselves, not God.

Nowadays, we can follow a non-religious moral code that doesn't require any middleman (God or religious belief)—and we can still be good, content, and thriving people. We can help people just because we are good people, without any God or religion being involved.

Children are the most susceptible to religious indoctrination. Repetitive church services and incantations and recitations embed nonsense into undeveloped minds. Kids are very credulous and have undeveloped frontal cortexes. They will believe pretty much anything their parents and educators tell them, especially if it is repeated enough. It is extremely wrong to lie to them. Eventually, most kids come to realize that the Tooth Fairy, Santa Claus, and unicorns are not real. Fairy tales go the way of the dodo bird. And the same should happen with God, although the best thing would be to not teach them about God at all. Learning about history, including about religious systems, is recommended. Key figures within the religions such as Jesus, Mohammed, Moses, Abraham, etc., are interesting to learn about. Ancestral stories can be educational. But with growing up and maturing (and development of frontal cortex), it needs to be made clear that God, similar to goblins and ghosts, is not a real thing. Although I agree completely with Richard Dawkins in his science and his frustration over religions brainwashing kids, I believe militant atheism is not the answer to this. The quiet voice of reason, spoken over and over, will do more to encourage people to think for themselves. I want this book to be one of the voices for reason. I do agree fully with Dawkins' view of schooling—religion should absolutely not be allowed in publicly funded schools. If people want their children to attend a religious school, they should have to pay full costs for that. They can have their imaginary God, religion/cult and practice it, but not at tax-payers' expense. I would hope that more religious adults would read this book and think about these recommendations for their own children and grandchildren.

RELIGION, IDOLATRY, AND PROPHETS[42]

Although Jews and Muslims do not worship any person, Christians do. Jesus Christ was an embodiment of God to the Christians. Christians created the "trinity" – a complicated new story for explaining their God. Jesus was a person who strove to show a good way of living. He was a role model and was

---

constructed into a messiah by the Christians. He was a Jew yet the Jews viewed him as a teacher but definitely not God. Many of his teachings were good. He certainly shook up the status quo, which was good for the times he lived in. He gave hope to many outcasts, poor people, and slaves. He certainly had some positive messages that were needed for his times. But it's very dangerous to believe that one person had such power and was so perfect in so many ways. That he was God's son on Earth is really stretching the imagination, to say the least. Worship of a non-existent God is bad enough; idolizing a person is arguably worse. Humans, especially 2000 years ago, had such a high need for hope for a better future, that they created a very elaborate story about a trinity, and made an idol out of a probably very zealous and charismatic person (messianism). However, Christian, Muslim, and Jewish myths were based on myths originating much earlier in Egypt, Mesopotamia, and Asia. Christianity was just cherry-picking from the past to create a new twist on old themes. Prophecies and revelations are equally questionable. Pretty much anyone could have a prophecy or revelation—the presentation (marketing of the idea) is what is going to make or break how many people buy in. It is said that in Jesus' time there were at least twenty other "messiahs" around. One would think in year 2020, it would be obvious that revelations and prophecies were just other ways of selling ideas, most of which never came/come true. And actually, ask yourself this: have any of those Bible prophecies and revelations come true? When Jesus appeared, the time was ripe for change. Older Roman and Greek polytheism had started to dwindle. It was very disjointed and expensive to support many gods' temples and shrines. There were many circumstances that allowed this new religion to gain popularity, amongst them was a monotheistic triune God who became human. This was quite a creative and fantastical new twist on older themes.

This is not to negate in any way the importance Jesus has had in history, but instead recognizes that, from a perspective 2000 years later, many questions arise. Jesus' story has serious limitations. For example, if Jesus were alive today, would he be considered to have a mental illness? Possibly he had schizophrenia, which is a mental disorder characterized by the inability to act or think in a rational way, as well as having delusions. Even if it was not a mental illness, his ideas were certainly extremist (promises of salvation and revelation). The stories of the magic and miracles he performed are simply not believable. People often project their own wishes on a person and idolize that person, despite some very serious flaws. If we acknowledge that Jesus was a real human being, then we know that he would *not* have been perfect just as every other human being is not perfect. Using statistics, the odds that he was God are so low, that essentially, the odds of Jesus being (a) God are *zero*.

Many try to defend the Bible stories as symbolic/metaphorical and think that nonbelievers cannot grasp what is being symbolized. This is not true. Nonbelievers realize these concepts are important to know about *historically* (symbols and elaborate imaginations and fables), but not necessary now. The passing on of ancestral stories and distilled truths are interesting; however, the negatives (the horrendous violent behaviours) far outweigh the positives for keeping such stories a central part of our lives. When young kids are taught about Jesus' crucifixion, would this not be terrifying for a young mind? Is that what Christians are trying to do? Terrify people into submission? How do we as a society promote goodness and kindness when the absolute perfect Christian man (Jesus) was tortured and murdered in such a horrendous way? And to use the abstraction of "God's son on earth"—really does stretch the imagination to the point of ridicule. The concept of "ultimate sacrifice" is understood, but the portrayal is absolutely objectionable. As mentioned before, since humans evolved to survive in groups, it follows that most parents would gladly give up their own lives to save their own children's lives. No god involved. The complexity that Christianity supposedly contains is perplexing. Why would people be looking to add more complexity in their lives, when most people could benefit from simplifying and refining their lives as much as is possible in our complex societies? Staying with simple truths, as listed in the morals and virtues section, is enough for most humans, especially in this increasingly complex world.

We have some more recent role models that would be more appropriate to acknowledge, such as Gandhi, Stephen Hawking, and Bill Gates, but at least with these exceptional people, we do not pretend that they were or are perfect or God's son on Earth. To put a human being on a pedestal is a very bad idea—inherent in that idea is the probability that this person will most likely fall down and can never live up to the idea of perfection. However, of course, that is the irony about Jesus followers today—they have the advantage to say that Jesus was perfect and the son of God, and we nonbelievers will never know because somehow, they know exactly what happened 2000 years ago, but we do not.

There is a popular public intellectual in Canada who has been interviewed about whether Jesus was the son of God and went to heaven and whether the Buddha reached nirvana. He stated that yes, probably these two people, *in the history of all mankind,* probably did reach heaven/nirvana. This person is also very keen on the importance of archetypes in mythology and religions with respect to their ongoing importance in human societies today (this has been his area of study for 30 years so it's understandable why he would think that). He prides himself as a critical thinker and states as much in many of his talks and interviews. But think about the probability of this—what are the odds that, out of all humans ever born on this earth, that only two of them (who must have been exceptionally special) reached heaven/nirvana or a state of perfection, for sure? The odds of this being true are so extremely low, so low that they would be next to zero. But this PhD professor, says that he is willing to believe that this could be true. He is willing to accept that 0.0001 % chance that this event of reaching heaven/nirvana/perfection could have happened. It is true that there is an infinitely small chance (next to zero) that this happened. But really? Think about the odds. I'm not buying those odds.

And then people such as this, if you question them, will tell atheists that we miss the point of symbolism, concepts, metaphors, and archetypes. That we don't get it—that these are examples of idols/heroes/ideals to aspire to. That these are human narratives/stories showcasing important concepts that humans grapple with. I think there would be better ways to show goodness and morality other than praising human sacrifice, which is ultimately, the story of Jesus. Crucifixion, torture, misogyny, violence, slavery and war, are *not* what I want to be focusing on in the twenty-first century. The concept of sacrifice is understood, but it's not necessary to continually repeat stories of extreme sadism.

This example reflects the massive pull that extremist-type stories contained within religious systems have. Many people are willing to overlook the statistics, the odds against this being true, just to hold out hope that indeed, there is a god, and there is a heaven. This was the 0.0001% chance person, a PhD psychologist, who is on record on YouTube. And this is what he is saying. Clearly, he has been very personally influenced by religion, and is susceptible to illogical thinking just like everyone else is. Even though he surely understands statistics, he might just have a very big personal blind spot with regard to religion, and my guess is that many, many people are the same. This is a great example of *confirmation bias*, which is making information fit your beliefs.

Some of the foundational/archetypal stories humans have, such as the creation myth, the hero and warrior myths, and the virgin-impregnation myth are interesting. Certainly, they have affected human evolution, and may indeed be embedded within our collective human psyches/consciousness. After *eons of distillation*, there are truths (as set out in the morals and virtues section) that exist. However, continually referring back to bible stories as justifications or explanations for current bad behaviours (wars, conflicts, racism, bigotry, misogyny) is unacceptable. Yes, humans have these narratives, but we are also able to rise above base instincts and use reason and logic to see them for the myths that they are. We have seen that humans *can* be capable of better and more evolved behaviour, such as living peacefully in pluralistic societies such as Mauritius, Japan,

India, Canada, the USA, and Western-European countries. It is not easy, but it can be done. Idealistic, yes. Worthwhile, yes.

It is possible to go beyond these tribal stories, and it is much more beneficial as a human species to choose positive and forward versus negative and backwards. As an explanation for describing behavior historically, these myths and stories are useful, but beyond that, we can strive to be better and to reach our human potential by keeping base instincts in check. As individuals, communities, and globally, we can do better than being trapped in the past.

> "*We have Christians against Muslims against Jews, and no matter how liberal your theology, merely identifying yourself as a Christian or Jew lends tacit validity to this status quo. People have morally identified with a subset of humanity rather than with humanity as a whole.*"
> Sam Harris

RELIGION AND POLITICS—THE UN INTERNATIONAL COURT OF JUSTICE[43]

We are supposed to have separation of church and state in our Western democracies, yet I often hear politicians using religion in their arguments. Very often, I hear "God Bless America"—well

---

43   www.icj-cij.org

what God/whose God? The Western world was generally settled by Europeans of Judeo-Christian heritage. But now there is a multitude of ethnicities and religious backgrounds throughout the Western world. Certainly, when Christian settlers came to North America, there was much harm done to the First Nations peoples, such as the history of the residential school abuses. The legacy of religious indoctrination and subordination is still leaving lasting problems. Christians certainly believed that their belief system was superior to that of the indigenous populations. This was an example of proselytizing to the natives. That's another example in terms of Christianity thinking they have superior answers to how to live in the world. It's simply not true and people now in the world need to view other cultures as different, but not superior or worse than themselves. The evidence of indigenous trauma (sexual, psychological, and cultural), speaks for itself. Reconciliation and reparations are ongoing between the settlers and the First Nations. The street is two-way, however, and both sides need to see each other as contributors to the problems, but also to the solutions. We all have to get along in this world, as a first principle, which is the basis for Humanism. Perseverating on the past is serving neither party well. Acknowledge that major grievances and harms were carried out against the First Nations peoples, but now they, as well as the descendants of the settlers, need to move forward as co-residents on the land together as positively as possible.

Interestingly, some of the American founding fathers were clearly complete secularists and skeptics. Thomas Jefferson and Abraham Lincoln strongly questioned the existence of God. James Madison (aka The Father of the Constitution, and the fourth president of the USA), insisted on the separation of church and state. However, over time, it is apparent that God-creep has infiltrated politics again. We need to do better as individual citizens to engage in politics, and demand that religion not be allowed to play any role whatsoever in the public political sphere.

Regarding religion and politics, politicians are savvy in knowing they can play into the divisions that religions naturally create for themselves. Religion and politics engage the feeling/emotional brain. Politicians use religion to manipulate and control different groups. For examples, look no further than the Evangelicals, the "theocons" (theological conservatives), the "alt-right" (alternative right), and populist movements in some countries. Shamefully, they use religion as an excuse to spew hatred or extreme dislike about certain groups of people—often ethnic or other religious minorities. Even though some "good" Christians, Muslims, or Jews might believe this is not how religion should be used, the *reality* is that often it *is* used in this way to polarize groups of people by focusing on their differences and not their common humanness. It is a very crude way to play into people's fear of otherness (xenophobia). It seems humans continue to be susceptible to this manipulation. We need to use our thinking brain (rational, higher-level) to get beyond this.

As a prime historical example, Hitler polarized his people against a created enemy. He used the Jews as scapegoats for all sorts of economic troubles. The results were absolute devastation and horror. How could people fall for this? But there are politicians now who are speaking in a similar manner to how Hitler spoke—blaming others and scapegoating minority groups. How can we avoid this currently? Firstly, by simply acknowledging and recognizing that we as humans are susceptible, we can go above this primitive way of viewing the world. By using our higher-level executive-thinking brains, we can make reasonable decisions. That humans all come from a common African ancestor—this is the main thing to focus on; not how we evolved to have some physical and belief-system differences. Tribal ways of thinking do not serve the world well in the twenty-first century.

There is currently a trend towards populism and nationalism in many developed countries. There is fearmongering by politicians and religious leaders who want to keep the status quo. They want to hunker down, to protect their borders and their people from job losses. This is actually the wrong approach. In the short term, it may be very painful for jobs to be eradicated or replaced by different types of jobs. But in the long run, it is the only way to move forward and evolve societally, economically, and globally. The key to all of the changes that need to happen eventually is *excellent transition planning*. Nothing should be done "cold turkey," nor would it be feasible for anything to happen overnight. Before changes are implemented, the best leaders need to be employed in making the best possible transition plans. Plan, plan, plan, then implement. That is what we are not seeing enough of with our elected leaders currently. Looking ahead and anticipating what is going to be needed to make the economy continue to function well is imperative. We must demand that our leaders show us good economic transition plans. And new jobs, systems, and infrastructure need to be in place before jobs are deleted or industries shut down.

The exchange of ideas that accompany goods is an antidote to the bigotry and hatred encouraged by demagogues. This, again, is manipulation by preying on people's feelings and emotions (fear of job loss, fear of others—foreigners) just like religious leaders do. Once again with science—it doesn't matter where the discoveries, inventions, and creations come from—if it's good for mankind, then let's share the idea. Religion has no part to play in any of this progress. In fact, with its inherent bigotry and divisive nature, religion is anti-progress.

Regarding immigration—rules do need to be followed to make it fair. Crossing borders illegally is not ok. Border systems are not equipped to manage huge numbers of people arriving en masse, wanting refuge. Even though desperate people take desperate measures, everyone needs to follow the rules for societies to work well. A middle-way or balanced approach should be used. Nations do need to be able to manage human migrations, but within reason. Ideally, people would not have to seek refuge from war or persecution by fleeing their own country. This is where global organizations such as the UN can help. Helping people stay in their own countries and providing humanitarian help in areas of conflict/violence is crucial. There needs to be continued international pressure to decrease violence, war, and persecution of minorities. And one of the main ways to doing this is by formally demoting religion to the lowest possible priority and putting humanitarian (Humanism) effort as number one.

> "Racism is on its deathbed—the question is, how costly will racists make the funeral?"
> Martin Luther King

> "The only thing that permits human beings to collaborate with one another in a truly open-ended way is their willingness to have their beliefs modified by new facts. Only openness to evidence and argument will secure a common world for us."
> Sam Harris

The UN's international court of justice (The Hague, Netherlands) is key in showing the whole world that certain human-rights standards are expected and will be enforced. There will be many who criticize this court, but think about this—Is it still not better to have international communication and collaboration and leaders talking than to have no court at all? There are problems with countries committing human-rights abuses with no apparent consequences. No question. However, the world is watching. Diplomacy, keeping the peace and avoiding war are also extremely important. There is much to work to be done toward getting all nations to follow human-rights standards.

Regarding emigration and travelling, generally, it is very beneficial to have exchanges of peoples from different places—this is how ideas are exchanged and transformed, and peace is maintained. Once you know and learn about people from different countries, you are less likely to want to kill them. Travelling is an incredible experience for learning about different people, places, and things. It also tends to be very bonding—in that people realize that we humans are really pretty much the same no matter where we live. All humans need food, shelter, and clothing. How we all go about meeting these needs is very interesting indeed. Learning about art, architecture, and history in a different part of the world goes a long way toward enlightening our minds, and gaining appreciation for other cultures. Realistically, travel, exchanges of information, and collaborating with other nations are going to be the way to go as opposed to digging in heels and staying separate (closing borders) and stuck in the old ways. Most people who are fearful of foreigners or people different from themselves have never been exposed to different cultures. That is why travel and cultural exchanges are critical for humans. School programs that include cultural exchanges are imperative for young people to learn about other ways of living. Political leaders who have the collaborative, expansive approach, are completely preferable to those who promote protectionism, closed borders, and closed minds.

Economically, history informs us that free trade is generally the best way to go for human flourishing. The best antidote to tribalism, nationalism, and warfare is free trade. Historically, when trade is flowing freely without a lot of government protectionism (tariffs, supply-chain management), times have been peaceful and economies flourish. When people are fearful (and prompted by politicians and union leaders that they should be scared for their industry or jobs), they dig in their heels and don't want to move philosophically, physically, or mentally. The potential for losing your job is indeed a very frightening prospect. However, recognizing that free trade in the long run generally leads to better, wealthier economies, people need to know that transition plans for evolving economies are going to be key to a prosperous future.

This is apparent in many countries today—with the global concern for climate change, people are demanding that fossil fuels use be stopped immediately. There is no way that is feasible or reasonable right now. People also need to be reminded of the major role fossil fuels have played in allowing humans to evolve their societies. Coal, oil, and gas were (and are) major economic drivers, which allowed human societies to thrive and develop (heat, warm running water, cars, factories). Fossil fuels are not the enemy—they have pulled more people out of poverty and misery than can be numbered. The real problem is that there are *too many people* overall on the planet requiring energy (especially true in China and India when total global emissions are looked at). If humans would show more restraint in reproducing, the world would not be in such a dismal state. This is why providing birth control to all reproductive age people worldwide is critical. It's going to be extremely important for *all* countries to develop alternate ways to provide energy to their populations. Nuclear energy must be seriously reconsidered in addition to tapering the amount of fossil fuels used in economic development. Of course, managing population numbers is hugely important but as I describe further on, women will naturally limit the numbers of children they have when they have consistent access to education, employment, birth control and vaccinations. The most important thing, within our governments, is to have very strong leadership on transition planning. The best people from industry and academia need to be engaged with evolving technologies, and planning in concrete terms what is needed exactly to transition away from fossil fuels. The people whose jobs will disappear need to have new jobs or training to go to. These job-training programs are going to be absolutely critical. The new systems need to be in place before shutting down old systems. The enemy is fear-mongering alarmists who do nothing to *actually solve the problems.* The problems are going to be solved by, once again, our great scientists, thinkers, and creators. Nuclear energy will have to be implemented (low risk) unless another way is created in the near future. Solar and wind have not proven effective as replacements to fossil fuels but can still play a role in reducing carbon emissions.

> *"When goods do not cross borders, soldiers will."*
> Bastiat

RELIGION, PUBLIC HEALTH[44] & GOVERNMENT SYSTEMS[45]

Religion does not have to play a role in public health other than to inform about peoples' backgrounds and cultural practices.

---

44   Turner, L. *Bioethics and Religions: Religious Traditions and Understandings of Morality, Health and Illness.* Health Care Annals. 2003.

45   Pew Research Center. *Religion and Government.* Fact Tank. 2017. & *How Religious Restrictions Have Risen Around the World.* 2019.

However, it is important to understand populations' religious beliefs to help inform programs. A mantra for public health promotion could be: *education, vaccination, and birth control.* As noted previously, religion is frequently against these ideas (science). But as far as pulling the world up from poverty, disease, and overpopulation, public health measures win over religion every time. In developing countries, as market economies are introduced and people have more opportunities to get educated, work, and obtain birth control, they often choose to have fewer children. Vaccination helps more children survive; parents don't need to keep having children if the ones they have will survive. As well, parents generally want surviving kids to get educated, so they will put more resources into fewer children. In general, being employed naturally limits how many children a family can take care of. The overpopulation issue will (theoretically) solve itself when market economies spread throughout the world and poverty decreases. The world's population will likely top out around 10-11 billion.[46],[47]

A fantastic public health (humanism) example of great innovation is when the Bill Gates Foundation organized a competition to solve the sewage/sanitation/hygiene issues in developing countries such as India. Currently many children die young from infection due to contaminated water. The system for

---

46   Pew Research.org

47   www.un.org

handling sewage is open-pit style or anyplace on the street, basically. This means raw sewage mixes with drinking and washing water, infecting many. Poor sanitation ties in with the higher birth rates in developing countries. When sanitation systems, along with vaccines, birth control, and education are provided, women tend to have fewer children. All these factors are related to each other in terms of better health outcomes. Free trade and free-market economies generally lead to wealth increasing and spreading across the globe—increasing job opportunities within the developing countries. Investing in health globally is absolutely necessary because, as market economies develop, they require a healthy population to work in them.

By setting up a competition, great ideas can be generated. Some of the waste/sanitation centres that arose from Gates' competition now are being used in places such as India and South Africa where putting in sewers and traditional sanitation systems is just not feasible. This is a fascinating project of immense global importance and shows true caring about the globe and all of its people. In terms of health, happiness, and peace, it is obvious that helping fellow humans wherever they might be is beneficial for the whole planet. We, as wealthy societies, have moral obligations to the whole planet—as more people are pulled up from poverty, they can flourish and contribute to their economies.

Of note about reason and balance vs politics and economics—as a thread that runs through this book, is the idea of *balance*. History has shown that *neither extreme capitalism nor communism/socialism work well*. Whether some leaders like it or not, the health, wealth, and happiness indices of nations show that the best economic systems have some combination of both capitalism and socialism (public education and health in Scandinavian countries). As an example, the USA is very capitalistic and has generated immense wealth. However, when health indicators show that USA infant mortality and obesity levels are significantly higher, and that life expectancy is significantly lower than the best country's outcomes (Iceland), and as compared to thirty-five other OECD countries (Organization for Economic Cooperation and Development), it might indicate that their social programming (education and health care) needs revision. One factor that must be considered when comparing Scandinavian countries with ones such as the USA or Canada is geography. Whereas smaller countries can run a national health service more readily, it is difficult for very large countries to have the same level of coordination, consistency, and probably efficiencies. The USA and Canada are huge countries with massive regional differences. Comparative health studies have to include such factors when determining exactly what type of system will best serve their own population. That doesn't mean that we should not learn from good examples that are working pretty well. This is why continual health and education data analyses on large scales (comparing countries, cities and states/provinces) is necessary. Coordination amongst regions, cities, and countries is preferable compared to operating in silos of isolation.

History has shown how disastrous communism/complete socialism can be (for example, Stalin's Russia). Their potential for corruption and oppression is immense. The great minds, thinkers (creators and inventors), and businesspeople are stifled, with no motivation to achieve or improve. Ambition is killed. It is the ultimate recipe for societies collapsing and losing wealth, happiness, and health. Humans do not thrive in this environment. It is anti-human in that it kills potential. Capitalism can bring out the best in people in terms of innovations, wealth creation, and progress, but it can also leave some people completely in the dust. That is why a very basic public health and education system is needed to ensure that the most vulnerable and disadvantaged people have opportunity to rise in their lives and are not left in neglect, and that the variance between the extremely rich and the extremely poor is not massive. It is the *opportunities to rise* that are essential (the goal not being equality of outcomes but equality of access to education, health care, employment). Barriers to access of essential services such as education and health care need to be continually assessed and improved. That does not mean giving people a free ride, but rather opening up opportunities for marginalized communities. This is where public health data analyses (taxation, income, education levels, and other demographic indicators) come in and are critical when making economic policy decisions that will affect education and health systems.

The extremely rich should be *highly* encouraged to give back to society, as sometimes truly it was not their genius or abilities that allowed for the creation or inheritance of immense wealth (although sometimes it really is). Sometimes it actually is a situation of right place, right time for success to happen. Bill Gates is a wonderful example of giving back with incredible, innovative solutions to real-world problems in global health (such as the public sanitation/hygiene issues, and malaria and polio eradication in the developing world). He has also been quoted as saying that he's "pretty much an atheist," and belief in a God "makes zero sense." As an example of a person who has truly changed the world for the better with his creations (as Microsoft Corporation founder), who gives back to society, and is a *compassionate capitalist*, he's a great role model. He is also encouraging other very wealthy people to contribute more to societies[48].

Taxing the wealthy more and more is not necessarily the answer to re-distribution of wealth. When the rich feel they are being

---

48   www.givingpledge.org

targeted to give back disproportionately, they often move their wealth out of their own countries or try to shelter it from taxation. Therefore, taxing the wealthy increasingly may leave them less incentive to give back to their own countries. And not only is there the wealth drain that can occur with high wealth taxation, but the brain-drain. If a person can get a better deal in another country for their business, skills, and/or education, they will leave unless it is financially favorable for them to stay. Encouraging innovation and wealth creation is ideal, but innovators, businesspeople, and creators need to feel welcome, encouraged, and rewarded in their own countries. However, if wealthy people are making millions and millions of dollars passively, this could be taxed very highly to help keep the variance between ultra-rich and poor smaller.

> *"The old must always make way for the new, and one thing must be built out of the ruins of another. There is no murky pit of hell awaiting anyone."*
> Lucretius (c. 95-55 BCE)

RELIGION AND PERSONAL RESPONSIBILITY[49]

We can no longer use the excuses of tradition, culture, and "It's how I was brought up." Unless we've been living in a cave or under a rock, where we don't read or see the world news, we know about the current state of Christianity, Islam, and Judaism. Within each of these, there are major problems. From the Catholic Church abuses, to the repressive Islamic states, to the problems in Israel vs. Palestine, we can't ignore reality. Each of us is responsible to ask ourselves—how can we improve? For those who believe in moderate religion, I have to strongly disagree. Why? Because then it's cherry-picking and gerry-mandering, meaning that we pick and choose what works at the time. And clearly, changes in religions have not solved the ongoing issues. If we continually have to change the boundaries within what the church doctrine allows/disallows, what is the point? The best solution is to discard all religions (recognizing this is never going to happen any time soon)! This would be a massive paradigm shift, and could change the world for the better. People can still choose to follow a religion, but they can do so with eyes wide open as they become more educated. **Humanism could be a world philosophy to follow.**

---

49   Pargament, K. et al. *Religion and the Problem-Solving Process: Three Styles of Coping.* Journal for the Scientific Study of Religion, 1988, 27 (1): 90-104.

Many people worry that if they give up their religious community, they will lose their moral framework or somehow, they will now be bad people. The church might have been their social network. You do not need church, religion, or a belief in God to be a good person. There are many good social groups outside of churches and religion. My recommendation is to lose the religion but keep up the good community work, and continue forward as humanists. Don't follow the crowd or follow in your parents' footsteps just because it's always been done that way. People need to actively assert and educate themselves through challenging and hopefully discarding, their current religion. Ask questions and don't stop until you find satisfactory answers. My guess is that religion cannot be satisfactory over the long-term, as the system has too many flaws and negatives.

Education in schools should be teaching comparative religions from a historical perspective, pointing out the evolution of rational thinking and the scientific method to students. A moral code and character development can also be taught in courses such as health and life skills or CALM (career and life management). With determination, teaching humanism, character and virtue development in schools (starting in preschool and continuing to grade 12) will become a norm just as healthy eating, physical activity, and mental health care are. And it can't just be an add-on or a minimal part of the curriculum. Morals and virtues teaching can be repeatedly taught throughout the learning years and re-iterated throughout life. These six pillars can be a starting point: trustworthiness, respect, responsibility, fairness, caring, and citizenship. Just as we are now teaching kids meditation, mindfulness, and healthy lifestyles, we can teach moral codes in school, at home, and in our communities. Spirituality can be included by teaching humanism, meditation, and mindfulness and encouraging volunteerism and contributing back to society in meaningful ways.

> *"Take the risk of thinking for yourself—much more happiness, truth, beauty, and wisdom will come to you that way."*
> Christopher Hitchens

SUMMARY OF ARGUMENTS AGAINST RELIGIONS

Up to this point all the negatives about religion have been discussed. But this book is supposed to be about positivity! This is what HAPPIER Humans is for—as an integrated health promotion model and a vision for the future. HAPPIER Humans (Humanism, Atheism, Positivity, Personal Responsibility and Enlightenment Ideals) can be used as a plan to follow for the different levels of personal, community, and global outlook. If we removed religion from peoples' minds, we could focus solely on helping others without trying to convert them to faith/god-belief, or wasting time on any superstitious activities.

What would the world be like without religion? It would be a better place—a place where humans see each other simply as other humans, and help each other (care, love, and compassion) just for that reason. It's that simple. And there is no need to invoke a god or other imaginary being. When we remove religion, we take away excuses to behave badly. Think about the whole world if we removed even three of the main religions (Christianity, Judaism, and Islam). We'd be removing the reason for war in a lot of the world. How's that for a good reason? It is idealistic and something to strive for. We need to remind the Jews, Muslims, and Christians that they all come from a common African ancestor and should be brothers and sisters versus enemies. That is why Humanism would work for everyone. It's not a religion, but a philosophy, or life approach, *suitable for all humans.*

For people who argue that humans have always had gods, I say that's nice. But the truth is that in our pre-tribal times, we likely just had talismans and stories. These eventually evolved to more elaborate gods, myths, and archetypes. As humans continue to evolve, we are gaining more and more knowledge to understand now that gods exist in imagination only. It's good to understand history because we should learn from it. If we examine the holy books of the three main religions, we realize they are filled with violence, war, racism, misogyny, and extreme and unbalanced views (the Old Testament in the Christian Bible, the Koran and Jewish holy books). They were useful when humans lived in tribes, and in the Middle Ages when they were uneducated and illiterate. But they are not useful now, other than as historical reference books. Why people cling to the past and their traditions and culture can be explained to some extent psychologically (see references on how human minds work). But take female genital mutilation and male circumcision as examples— just because these are cultural traditional norms does not make them ok or justified. Just because 2000 years ago it made sense to listen to our tribal myths, it doesn't make sense now. It's time to move away from that tribal mentality when we don't live in tribes anymore. We live in a highly complex, knowledge-based society now where tribal fables do not have much relevance. They may have been helpful to explain the past, and provide us with distilled truths, but now we need to strive to do better and focus on the positive aspects of human nature. We should not mire ourselves in the past.

Religion and Failure to Thrive: It is evident that dysfunctional countries that try to maintain regressive, religion-led governments fail in their happiness levels, as well as in other health indicators (Afghanistan, Iran, Saudi Arabia, Syria, Pakistan). Maintaining tribal mentality has kept these countries without scientific progress, and stuck in poverty. Although Saudi Arabia may have country wealth from their oil reserves, most of the people, especially women, are restricted in many ways. And it is telling that the elites in those countries often send their university-age students to the USA, Canada, and Western Europe to get educated. In ancient times, the Persian and Arabic countries were very progressive, and making scientific advancements. However, after militant Islam came, science and progress have been at a standstill, and most of the technologies are coming from the West. The repression of new and better ways within the regressive religious states show that humans cannot flourish in such an environment.

Even Christianity, which is supposed to have a caring, benevolent God, really has no evidence of this. Who/or what would actually sacrifice their own child (Jesus) in such a cruel torturous way? And he was a sacrifice for other people's sins—now think about that—does this make sense? Is this a good role model? No, it's horrible, extreme, and twisted. And there is the story about Abraham and his son Isaac, whom he was supposed to sacrifice to show his devotion to God, though in the end, he obeyed God, and didn't have to kill his son (it was just a test but a horrible, cruel test at that). However, do you know the story of Jephthah who does sacrifice his daughter to God as payment for victory in battle? Even two thousand years ago, this seems utterly, cruelly, and completely absurd. In the Koran, the non-believers of Islam will have their skin burned off in Hell and yet their skin will grow back only to be burned off again and again.

In parts of the Hebrew holy books, the tales of extreme violence, cruelty, and racism dominate.

If a person actually reads the Old Testament, the Torah, and parts of the Koran, the tales of torture, rape, killing, and extreme violence are many. This is not a good guide for anybody. Perhaps two thousand years ago, sacrifices and torture were a way of life and helped scare people into submission and desired behaviours. The Old Testament is full of animal sacrifices—did God ever like his sacrifices! Do we sacrifice animals and humans today? Excuse me if I'm really not seeing how all these sacrifices have any relevance today. There are lots of details about how to kill properly, but why keep reading and repeating tales that are basically brutal and awful? Many people are quick to condemn other ancient cultures (Aztecs, Mayans, Greeks, Vikings, Egyptians, Chinese) for human and animal sacrifice. However, Christianity is equally bad, if not worse, for what is the story of Jesus if not a story in praise of human sacrifice? It's extremely obscene really. And what is even more repugnant is the number of people today who have chosen to continue to follow this bizarre cult. Humanism could replace all religions.

Circa 2020, we do not live in that world, thankfully. In the most dysfunctional, depraved, deprived and *religious* places on Earth today (Afghanistan, Iran, Pakistan, Syria, Saudi Arabia), these tribal and biblical behaviors continue. These tales of horror are not something to focus on if we as humans want to become more peaceful, more caring, and more helpful. Know the history but move on. Fill your mind with positive stories and lessons that don't involve torture, violence, killing, rape, war, and plunder. Even if, in our "collective consciousness" we hold these myths and archetypes in our DNA, we need to move to higher level thinking. We are capable. Know the information, but move forward and don't get trapped in the past.

Other authors[50] have stressed the importance of archetypes in mythology. Christianity used many of the previous ancient myths to incorporate into its own narratives. Christianity was a new twist on old themes. What many people don't realize is that the different religions have common threads running through them. The creation myth, the re-incarnation myth, the virgin-impregnation myth, the warrior myth—all had been created long before in the ancient Egyptian, Mesopotamian, Greek, Roman, Indian, and Asian religions. Perhaps after learning this, one might realize that *one's own religion really is not special.* It shares a lot of commonalities with other myths, not to mention the ongoing current state of cherry-picking within the religions themselves. So many different sects and offshoots and divisions—it's pretty obvious that even the religious see problems within their own religions. Now that we have the benefit

---

50   Peterson, J.   *Maps of Meaning: The Architecture of Belief.*
      Routledge. 1999.

of history on our side, is it not time to review these recurrent themes and put them to rest? Again, history is important to know, but it doesn't mean that we should be stuck there.

To re-iterate, in most of the happiest and healthiest places in the world there is a high rate of non-religiosity/atheism. As people in developing and developed countries have increased access to knowledge /education and poverty is decreased, there is also a decrease in numbers of children born per family, which will in turn aid with the overpopulation problem in the world. With more and more people realizing that religion does not deliver what it promises, my hope is that more people will choose reason and science, as opposed to the superstitious promises from religion.

From an atheist's perspective, observing these conflicts from afar, I have to be honest–they seem unbelievable. That in two thousand years, we have not been able to overcome these religious obstacles is a serious disappointment. And I'm sure that when you are a Jew or Muslim living in these ancient tribal areas, you *feel* very differently, because your whole *emotional identity* is centred on being part of your tribe and culture. But from my vantage point and background, which is of mixed heritage and different religions, I can honestly say that I think I am in an advantageous position to comment and have insight into this. Because my parents came from different countries and ethnic backgrounds originally (and immigrated to Canada), I had to become very comfortable with not being partial to just one side. I had to develop a way to see both sides. In a way, I believe that if there is anything I can do from an outsider's point of view, it would be that I can promote the idea of pluralism being an advantage, not a negative. Canada, Western Europe, the USA, Mauritius, Japan, India, and some other countries are pretty good examples. They do have problems and are by no means perfect, but they have also shown that it is possible to live together peacefully. It's difficult but necessary to start with the premise that we must all get along with each other in the world if we are going to make this world work better (that is decreasing wars and conflicts and increasing health and happiness in all countries). And how to achieve this pluralism is by promoting market economies, strong public health and education systems, demoting religious identities to a very minor role, and seeing each other simply as humans. The leaders of all countries need to engage in higher-level thinking. Bringing in mediators/negotiators from outside countries, as they have done, can also promote resolutions on some of the issues.

This is where an international supervising body like the United Nations comes in. While it has many issues as an organization, it is still important to have national leaders conversing and communicating on key human areas of need. It would be great to see the UN endorse humanism (and the Humanist Manifesto) as a foundational document. It's actually pretty difficult to argue against it, because it holds at its core what is best for all human beings, not just certain groups. When there are religious differences, could not the main focus of such an organization be to educate people away from their religion, and just focus on humanism and humanitarian needs? As well, it must be made clear that religious belief cannot be used as an excuse for bad behaviour. Part of our duty in the developed world, is to educate people to use evidence-based programs, as opposed to any faith-based programs. Developed countries need to lead the way and educate others in less developed countries. Open or market economies spread ideas as well as goods, so it is hoped that the idea of humanism versus religion will flow around the world eventually. With international trade, people are exposed to many ideas and ways of being, and can see and choose for themselves what makes the most sense.

In the UN, it should be stressed that science and reason are primary, and superstitious belief systems (religions) are not acceptable as reasons for negative behaviour. Human rights abuses need to be addressed and sanctioned by the international community. Evidence, observation, and empiricism (knowledge-based data) will be used. Teaching those in developing countries best practises based on scientific proofs is the optimal way to go. Focusing on common humanity is the way forward. Focusing on real issues such as vaccination, education, and birth control in developed and developing countries will make the difference in people's lives in a real, measurable way. This is humanism.

What if people simply helped other people because they want to? Not because a Bible, Torah, or Koran command it, but because they are simply human, and have an innate sense of human decency. Some will argue that a human moral code starts with a religious belief system, but this is *completely false*. Humans have evolved to be both helping and warring. Being of higher intelligence than other species, we have the ability to reason that helping others is much more beneficial than killing them, and keeping peace is in the world's best interests. In other words, a moral code is innate in humans. To bring up infants we need to nurture them. This is a basic human instinct. We take care of others. We only war when we focus on differences between peoples. However, humans are all human regardless of where they live. Focusing on the common humanness is the centre of humanism.

SECTION 4

SOME QUESTIONS TO ASK YOURSELF

Why is it that we don't see miracles and magic today like those written about in the Bible/Torah/Koran?

Would the Christian God do miracles and magic for the Muslim and Jewish people?

Whose God is right? Different religions are convinced their God is the right one.

People of each religion seem to believe they are special and are the chosen people. How could this be possible?

If the Christian god is all-knowing and all-caring, how can he allow so much suffering in the world?

What is God's plan when he allows a child to die from cancer?

The problem of unanswered prayers:

- people die despite prayers

- suffering continues despite prayers

- why would a benevolent, omnipotent God allow this?

- why are some countries rich and others poor?

- why does God continue to let children starve and allow diseases to kill?

- have the prophecies and revelations stated in the holy books come true?

Are you willing to bet on these odds?

- The probability of revelation is next to zero.

- The probability of a resurrection is next to zero.

- The probability of re-incarnation is next to zero.

- The probability of an after-life is next to zero.

DID YOU KNOW?

1. Religions are *not unique*. There are recurrent superstitious themes throughout modern religions (Judaism, Christianity, Islam) that originated much earlier in ancient cultures (such as Mesopotamian, Egyptian, Greek and Roman, Asian[51]):

---

51   National Geographic. *Essential Visual History of World Mythology*. 2008.`

- mythical creatures (Leviathan, Tiamet, Lotan, Behemoth)

- blessings, curses, sacrifices

- monsters, dragons, serpents, sorcerers, wizards, witches, seers, fortune tellers

Judaism, Christianity, and Islam are *not unique*—they kept borrowing and changing the story that would fit for the time and place—some of their stories might still carry over to modern times, but most don't. Religion goes against all educated, logical, and scientific reasoning. If you are interested in why people choose atheism versus believing in God—just read the *entire* Bible, Torah, or Koran!

2. Despite how certainty feels, it is neither a conscious choice nor a thought process. It is a trick of our brains based on evolutionary adaptation for individual and group survival. This is when the brain automatically operates, as in breathing. It is our primitive, intuitive, emotional/feeling brain operating—a fight or flight response that happens instantaneously. Our brains have evolved to detect threats and naturally look for problems and patterns. Although very well adapted to our prehistoric lifestyle of hunting and gathering, the sensitivity of the human brain is such that it often will detect threats nowadays, even when there are none. Our tendency towards vigilance and threats served us well in hunting

and warring scenarios—currently not as much, although the ability to detect threat is still important to us.

Certainty, and "knowing what we know," arise out of involuntary brain mechanisms, that, like love or anger, function independently of reason (neurosurgeon Robert A. Burton's book—*On Being Certain: Believing You are Right Even When You are Not*). Much like an impulse, the immediate reaction of your brain is to ensure your survival (fight or flight). In tribal warfare, instantaneous decisions were really important. Nowadays, we're usually not trying to outrun a sabretooth tiger or an arrow, so we are better off taking a PAUSE. To be really certain, we must pause and think for higher-level reasoning to operate; an instantaneous emotional reaction can often lead to bad decision making. Human brains are primed to want certainty. This is another reason religious systems have worked so well historically. They present themselves as authoritative truths, but they are really not. Nothing can be a hundred percent certain in this world. There is always a chance, however small, that what we are certain we know, is not true. We must keep this idea in our minds when we go to think about different subjects. Although we'd like certainty as humans, we have to realize and accept that nothing is absolutely certain. This idea requires us to use our higher-level thinking as opposed to relying on our instantaneous impression of certainty. The holy books' stories were written and presented in the certainty sense—which upon reflection and analysis, we now know is not very valuable.

Much has been written about the human brain and how it operates. I encourage you to read and learn more (see reference list).

QUESTIONS AND ANSWERS

Is this book an attack on religion?

I prefer to say this is an argument against *any superstitious or supernatural belief system*, which would include all religions. It is not an attack on any one religion, but rather against all supernatural belief systems.

What about all the good that churches do?

I'll never negate the good that churches/religions have done. The problem with churches/religions carrying out good deeds is that most of the time they also proselytize, meaning they try to convert the recipients of the charity to their religion. This is abhorrent, even though these church people believe they have good intentions. I call it out as brainwashing. The same happens in faith-based schools. The children have no choice in the nonsense that is fed to them. It's a form of indoctrination/brainwashing and can carry long-term negative psychological damage for some kids. There are many horrible stories about kids attending Catholic[52] (and other faith-based) schools and churches. The number of sexual abuse scandals that have rocked the Catholic Church leaves no room for denial. History shows corruption in the church clergy, basically from the start of Christianity. It is likely no different in Islam or Judaism, because any powerful institution that does not have outside oversight, monitoring, and evaluation is prone to corruption and abuse. Religious systems are not, at the core, democratic institutions. Other cults also have their horror stories—Jehovah's Witness, Mormons; the list goes on and on.

I also believe that in order to preserve the constitutions' charter of rights and freedoms, that is to practice one's religion freely, that faith-based schools can continue to operate if they are *entirely* privately funded. No state monies should be given to any faith-based organizations including schools. Faith-based organizations getting subsidies in the form of tax breaks should not. Think about all the money that could be redirected from churches towards other humanistic programs (education, health). Often the religious back anti-science, anti-women ideologies such as anti-abortion campaigns and creationism taught in school curriculums.

---

52   Grant, T. *The walking wounded: In Canada, survivors of Catholic Church sex abuse await a reckoning.* Globe and Mail article. September 24, 2019.

Lastly, I maintain that good charitable work can be done without religion. People are already coming together in such clubs as Rotary, Lions, Shriners, Doctors Without Borders, Girl Guides, Scouts, community organizations, and schools. Religion and churches are not necessary to be a good, kind, giving, and spiritual person with a meaningful life.

What would become of all the churches if religion was gone?

The churches do not have to be demolished. Re-use and re-purpose the buildings. In fact, my suggestion would be to transition the churches to *community humanist (health and education) centres*. I realize this is a pipe dream, but I see it as a possibility down the road of human evolution. This will never happen in my lifetime, but that doesn't mean I can't be a spark that tries to light that fire. Humanist centres could be gathering places doing much of the same good work as churches might currently do, but without the auspices of superstition/Church/religion. The International Humanists' Association has resources on how to do this (how to start a humanist centre). Their website is: www.humanists.international. Another great place for humanistic health and education services could be public libraries. Let's utilize the infrastructure already in place. Many people like to belong to clubs. There are so many to choose from—the centres could be used to host service clubs, book-clubs, boys' and girls' clubs, homework clubs, senior's activity centres, community kitchens and gardens, mom and tot, music/choir, fitness—pretty much anything. Libraries and churches (humanist community centres) could host interesting and educational talks by knowledgeable people (psychologists, medical doctors, lawyers, accountants, teachers, etc.) on a wide variety of topics, with the goal of promoting personal and *community engagement*, health, and wellness. Global initiatives could also be addressed using humanistic principles.

Why are you so against religion?

The most peaceful nations are the most secularized. The happiest countries are also the least religious. From a public-health perspective, the more religious the country, the unhealthier the populations. Gapminder.org and Steven Pinker's books give many statistics supporting this assertion. In general, the healthiest countries as indicated by health outcomes such as infant mortality, healthy mothers, clean water, vaccination rates, educational and employment attainment for the whole population (includes basic literacy up to post-graduate degrees) occur in the least religious countries (Denmark, Sweden, Norway, Finland, Czech Republic, Japan, Canada). Religious states such as Afghanistan, Iran, Pakistan, Syria, and Saudi Arabia have much worse health indicators. The highest murder rates also happen in the most religious nations and states, as do violent conflicts.

Perhaps a little history is helpful to help explain this. During the French Revolution (and this happened in many other countries as well, but the French Revolution was crucial in initiating world-wide changes)—1789-1799—the French monarchy was overthrown, and a republic was established. The monarchy had claimed Divine Right—rule by God through the king. People rightly saw this as horribly wrong, as it gave the monarchy freedom to do whatever they wanted at the expense of everyday people. (*Les Miserables* tells the story of the starving peasants revolting as the monarchy was conspicuously consuming). Through the revolutionary wars that started to happen around the world during and after the French Revolution, hard-won individual rights and freedoms were established.

The establishment of a *secular and democratic republic* became the new standard that other countries that wanted to evolve from monarchy rule, aspired to. There were many difficult and horrendous issues along the way, but the hard-won freedoms for the common person were never going to go away. When we look at the USA, we see a similar republic. Canada is based on a constitutional monarchy, but really the monarchy has no power except as figureheads/celebrities. This all, of course, is a gross oversimplification, but in this book, I'm trying to get down to the essential facts. Essentially, the masses resented the privilege and wealth that the monarchy and the Catholic clergy had, while the common man was actually starving. Out of the French Revolution came the *"Declaration of the Rights of Man and of the Citizen,"* and the abolition of feudalism and the privileges of the aristocracy. A huge accomplishment was the abolition of slavery. The Catholic Church was de-established, meaning it lost many of its previous powers. Throughout massive growing pains, many lives were lost in the subsequent uprisings of different factions (dictatorships during the reigns of terror).

Almost all other major upheavals in the modern era took their cue from the French Revolution. (The Russian, Chinese, Greek, Spanish Revolutions). These revolutions had the right idea of decreasing the powers of religion/churches and monarchies, especially at the government level, but their means of dictatorship, fascism, and communism were systems that failed miserably. It wasn't the abolition of religion that was the problem in these systems, but the form of government, replacing one bad system with another, although I must stress that I don't agree with forcing people to become atheist. This choice must be left up to individuals. It is a choice whether to believe in god and *there should be no coercion involved*. Forcing people to be atheist is equally as bad as forcing them to attest to a belief in god. Humanism is against coercion of any kind.

The French Revolution was actually intended to benefit the entire world especially the common, everyday people who make up the majority of the population. For this we have to thank history, for now in the Western world we have established individual rights and freedoms. It's hard to overstate how important this hard-won division of church and state is for us today. Democracies, as we know them, became the new standard to which many societies and countries aspire. Although democracies are far from perfect, most people in the Western world believe they are the best in the sense of being the fairest to most people.

How does politics relate to religion now?

In democratic, constitutionally-led countries, politics and religion are supposed to be completely separate. Does this actually happen though? No. Look at the USA—the presidents all seem to say, "God bless America." But the USA is an anomaly in the sense of religions. Many previous presidents were strongly secular-thinking and were very likely skeptics (Lincoln, Jefferson). But somehow, over the course of time, religious sects have grown increasingly influential. The reason for this is because religions are businesses. They exist to make money. These large church groups pay a lot of money to support politicians of their choice. American culture is highly individualistic and entrepreneurial—in other words, highly capitalistic. In general, this is a very good thing because it fulfills a lot of human needs such as self-actualization—making the life one wants. Far be it from me to be cynical, but I can only really see the money-making side of these huge evangelical and Christian cathedral churches. You have to admit that it's a pretty good business model—promising an incredible afterlife for attending and paying for spiritual saving. And what is spiritual saving anyway? Reaching Heaven? All the Church has to do is convince people that they will have a great life after death, but they don't have to prove it (nor could they if they tried)! Religion preys (pun intended) on people's weaknesses, wishful thinking, and susceptibility to things that sound too good to be true. Religion can be used as mean bully—conform to this belief system or you are forever damned. Abhorrent really. Hope should not be for sale, which it is in a church, essentially.

In a lot of countries, the leaders often bring in religion to sway opinion and win votes. This should not happen. Secular countries need to keep religion out of any public sphere, so as soon as I hear a leader mentioning God, a red flag goes up in my mind. I would never recommend voting for a religious person. Why not? It shows that they are illogical thinkers (or that they are willing to lie) and that is not what is needed for a good decision-maker and leader. If they are willing to lie to themselves and the public by believing in a non-existent god, then what else are they willing to lie about? Possibly a lot.

Can you talk a bit more about power in politics?

Whenever power is held undemocratically, social results are bad. Take a look at some of the worst historical regimes in the world: (most of these countries were also *highly religious and dysfunctional*).

> Uganda under Idi Amin
>
> Zimbabwe under Robert Mugabe
>
> Haiti under Baby Doc Duvalier
>
> Chile under Pinochet
>
> Iran under the Ayatollahs
>
> Spain under Franco
>
> The Philippines under Marcos
>
> South Africa under Botha's apartheid
>
> Germany under Hitler (supposedly a good Catholic)
>
> *USSR under Stalin's communism
>
> *Cambodia under Pol Pot
>
> *China under Mao's communism

*The last three were non-religious, but all leaders above were basically totalitarians/dictators and the leaders were *not* elected democratically.

You mentioned that health can improve in secular countries?

Previously I spoke about the French Revolution and what resulted from it. Along with the increased secularism in a country comes an increase in women's rights, status, health, and wealth. With secularism, sex education is not only allowed, but birth control is made available, so women actually have choice in when to get pregnant. It might not seem like much, but when health and medicine are kept separate from religious interventions, health measures improve. When women have control over their bodies, they can take more time to get training or an education that will help support them. When there are economic opportunities for women to work and gain wealth, they generally have fewer children, too, as most of them want to provide more in terms of education for each child they have. And working hours naturally limit the number of children it is feasible to take care of. *Health and educational improvements are positively correlated to secularization and decreased religiosity.*

A great current example of a role model is Malala Yousafzai (born 1997), the Pakistani activist, who is fighting for the rights of girls to get an education in Pakistan. She won the Nobel Peace Prize for human rights' advocacy in the NW territory where the Taliban (Islamic extremists) had banned girls from attending school. An attempt was made on her life for her activism, and she was forced to flee her country. Now she resides in England, and is an honorary citizen of Canada. The Taliban stated they were justified in their attempt to murder her for their religious convictions. She is now well-known internationally for the work she has brought to the forefront on the right to education for children. What a young role model she has become to people everywhere. Despite incredible forces arrayed against her (religious extremists), she has brought her voice of reason to the world. She is a great example of passion for reason and rights as opposed to religious dogma (she is Muslim, culturally).

You have a lot of arguments against religion— what do you propose instead?

Humanism. Instead of just negating current religious models that exist, I propose an improved model. I believe that a better model than churches would be to have **Humanist Centres** following the HAPPIER Humans model.

SECTION 5

FORESEEN CRITICISMS OF THIS BOOK AND CLOSING REMARKS

I visualized this book before I actually sat down to write anything. I wanted a *compact guidebook* that would fit the niche of general health promotion (self-help/personal development, and spirituality) with a large dose of real advice and facts to support my vision/model (happier humans). I did not want an academic tome that few would read. I'm aware my vision and model are *ideals* and not easily achievable given the world's current state.

I had already guessed that critics would describe my book as polemic, too simplistic, superficial, and reductionist. My response is that is exactly what I was aiming for, not in the sense of leaving out critical elements of each topic (humanism, atheism, positivity, personal responsibility, and ideals of the enlightenment), but to present only the core/essential information on each topic. I encourage readers to delve more deeply into each area discussed. Far from being simple, the topics are *much more complex and nuanced* than a guidebook allows. Ultimately this guidebook is to encourage readers to learn more by digging deeper into the topics individually.

As far as being an argument against religion, my book is exactly that, but not with the intent to disrespect others. I try to show an understanding of what it is in human nature that can lead people to follow a religion and keep them entrenched within it.

Another criticism might be that the content leaves out the "human touch"—the emotional and intuitive side of human nature and focuses too much on the reasoning, logical side. Again, my intent was to focus on the reasoning part of the brain as this is where best decisions can be made. If we are controlled more by the emotional side of the brain (more primitive), we can make sub-optimal decisions. Emotions may drive or initiate thought and feelings and are important to pay attention to, but ultimately, we need to use our higher brain functions for best choice-making. I encourage you to read more about emotional intelligence if you want to delve into that area.

Imagination, creativity, and the emotional side of human existence are very important and have a very big role to play in self-actualization and contentment. The architecture, art, and music in churches can be appreciated as showing amazing human abilities. Creating art and participating in the creative pursuits of music, dance, and theatre are all great. As long as we realize we need to keep a firm boundary between what is real and what is not, we're fine. And if we choose to go to church and believe in God, despite knowing no God exists, that's ok too—as long as we know we are choosing superstition, not reality. Some people like me will visit churches to appreciate the architecture and art, but don't believe in God. That doesn't mean that I don't respect the amazing creations of humans. I simply cannot live with a mental disconnect. The choice is yours to make for yourself.

The time for a new Enlightenment is NOW.

> *"The finest fury is the most controlled."*
> *"There can be no progress without*
> *head-on confrontation."*
> *"Exceptional claims demand exceptional evidence."*
> Christopher Hitchens
>
> *"Religion will recede not by atheists shouting*
> *condemnation, but by the quiet voice of reason slowly*
> *making itself heard."*
> Julian Baggini, 2003

The Baggini quote is one of my favourites—unfortunately I find it hard not to be very loud on this subject, but I hope, dear reader, you will consider the information put forward when you make your life choices.

In peace, health, and happiness (or shall I say "contentedness"), Ann Naimish

 Ann Naimish

DESIDERATA

Go placidly amid the noise and the haste and remember what peace there may be in silence. As far as possible, without surrender, be on good terms with all persons. Speak your truth quietly and clearly; and listen to others, even the dull and the ignorant; they too have their story. Avoid loud and aggressive persons; they are vexatious to the spirit. If you compare yourself with others, you may become vain or bitter, for always there will be greater and lesser persons than yourself. Enjoy your achievements as well as your plans. Keep interested in your own career, however humble; it is a real possession in the changing fortunes of time. Exercise caution in your business affairs, for the world is full of trickery. But let this not blind you to what virtue there is; many persons strive for high ideals, and everywhere life is full of heroism. Be yourself. Especially do not feign affection. Neither be cynical about love; for in the face of all aridity and disenchantment, it is as perennial as the grass. Take kindly the counsel of the years, gracefully surrendering the things of youth. Nurture strength of spirit to shield

you in sudden misfortune. But do not distress yourself with dark imaginings. Many fears are born of fatigue and loneliness. Beyond a wholesome discipline, be gentle with yourself. You are a child of the universe no less than the trees and the stars; you have a right to be here. And whether or not it is clear to you, no doubt the universe is unfolding as it should. Therefore, be at peace. And whatever your labors and aspirations, in the noisy confusion of life, keep peace. With all its sham, drudgery and broken dreams, it is still a beautiful world. Be cheerful. Strive to be happy.

(Max Erhman, 1927, but likely written significantly earlier than that by another person(s))

APPENDIX

POSITIVITY & PERSONAL RESPONSIBILITY (HAPPIER)

RECOMMENDATIONS FOR PERSONAL WELL BEING—INFORMATION KEY POINTS[53]

Positivity - attitude

- A healthy attitude of mind is the single most important factor in the promotion of health and prevention of disease. By a process of constant reiteration, a positive attitude must be made part of our habitual daily life.

- Sow and act and you reap a habit; sow a habit and you reap a character; sow a character and you reap a destiny.

A long and happy life is generally achieved by (and can be taught):

- Cheerful, optimistic attitude/disposition

- Positive outlook and approach

- Being alert and active

---

53 Seligman, Martin. *Flourish: A Visionary New Understanding of Happiness and Well-Being*. Simon and Schuster. 2011.

- Being adaptable

- Being needed and of being of use to society

Points on being happy/content/joyful and positive: (practising gratitude is essential for this)

- Happiness is a choice.

- Happiness comes from within.

- It is not a result of external circumstances.

- Realize that happiness may be fleeting (connected to circumstances), whereas joy comes from engaging with the world with a humanistic approach.

- Joy is the result of the culmination of "being," or the "good mood of the soul".

- Joy and gratitude can be described as spiritual practices.

Characteristics of Positivity

1. Commitment—highly motivated to attain clearly defined, self-appointed goals; a sense of purpose provides a reason to live and powerful motivation to stay alive; purposeful work—that is, giving meaning to life through useful work; work/rest cycles are necessary to achieve mental/physical balance as well as personal satisfaction and enjoyment; self-respect is earned through the journey and the process; from our successes we gain satisfaction, and from our failures we gain wisdom.

2. Calmness—most virtues become vices when practised to excess; we need to aim for serenity of mind, emotional composure, and a pervasive and persistent calmness of temperament (equanimity); several techniques can be used to acquire an attitude of calmness: rest pauses (daily, weekly, holidays); daily muscle relaxation; relaxing hobbies such as yoga, reading, etc.; soothing stimulation (classical music, massage, baths, etc.).

3. Confidence—hardiness and resilience; we need to feel in control of our lives; rules for this include: accepting full responsibility for your whole life; being yourself; setting reasonable goals; establishing control over your environment; gaining experience; acting "as if" you are confident. Gradually you will truly become confident through life experiences.

4. Conviviality (sociable and upbeat)—give to get; love yourself; cultivate friendships; make the effort to engage with other people; keep your friendships in repair; show kindness and caring; praise often, condemn rarely.

5. Optimism.

6. Cheerfulness—smile often; find time to play and have fun; don't take yourself or your life too seriously.

7. Contentment—the synthesis of mind and body; being patient; not rushing; live in the moment (not in the past or future); see life in historical perspective; move on

from errors in the past; learn to accept the inevitable (death and taxes).

Positive Thinking Techniques

1. Separate fact from fiction:

    a. Stop negative self-talk.

    b. Most of our negative thoughts are just that—thoughts, not facts.

2. Identify and label the negative thoughts on paper:

    a. When you see the words "never," "ever," "worst," "always," you can bet these statements aren't true.

    b. Whenever it feels like something is never/always, this is just your brain's natural threat-awareness tendency inflating perceived intensity or frequency of any event.

3. Replace the negative thought with a positive one:

    a. Think about your day and identify one positive thing that happened, no matter how small.

    b. Whenever you notice your mind wandering back to negativity, repeat the process of replacing the negative thought with a positive one.

VISUALIZATION = the Mental Rehearsal technique. This is the process of living the experience on the inside (your mind) before having it on the outside; attitude here consists of—interest, enthusiasm, expectancy and desire.

VAVA = Visualize, Affirm, Verbalize, Assume the Role.

Keep your thoughts, your conversations, your dreams, your imagination, and your feelings on what you want (not on what you don't want). Becoming a purely positive person requires desire, decision, determination, and discipline; you have to first and foremost define clearly who you want to be and what you want your life to look like; visualize yourself with a clear mental picture—the key is vividness of the picture; write down your goals in the present tense, close your eyes and visualize them as if they were accomplished; imagine the satisfaction/pleasure that you would feel if this was your reality.

TO PREVENT IMPULSIVE/KNEE-JERK/ *EMOTIONAL* REACTIONS TRY THESE TECHNIQUES:

HALT - Am I hungry, angry, lonely, or tired right now? This acronym helps to make you stop/pause for a minute to think about how you are feeling and what would be a good response.

RULER[54] (regarding emotional intelligence)

>R = recognize your feelings/emotion
>
>U = understand your triggers
>
>L = label your feeling/emotion
>
>E = express appropriately
>
>R = regulate your emotions

Positive Psychology = Personal Responsibility - How to achieve this (contentment and success)[55]?

1. Make a commitment.

2. Set goals.

   G-O-A-L-S - (Must write these down)

   Goal-oriented-action-leads-to-success

   Make your goals SMART.

   >S = smart
   >
   >M =measurable
   >
   >A=achievable
   >
   >R=relevant
   >
   >T=time-framed

3. Plan your work and work your plan (write it down).

4. Always do quality work (do your best).

5. Be personally responsible for your work.

---

54 Brackett, Marc. *Permission to Feel*. MacMillan. *2019*

55 Seligman, M. *Authentic Happiness: Using the new positive psychology to realize your potential for lasting fulfillment.* New York Free Press. 2002.

6. Cooperate.

7. Make an effort to contribute.

8. Persevere through tough times (perseverance, persistence, patience, and pride).

9. Communicate effectively.

10. Live with integrity.

11. Celebrate life. (Celebrating your own accomplishments helps to continue motivating you!)

12. Make learning a life-long habit.

13. Being Personally Responsible and Accountable (Think for yourself and make choices.)

14. C—consciousness

15. H—humour (always, always good!)

16. O—optimism

17. I—initiative

18. C—commitment

19. E—engagement

Use Affirmations/Make sure to remind yourself:

1. I am responsible for my happiness.

2. I am responsible for my choices and actions.

3. I am responsible for the way I prioritize my time.

4. I am responsible for the level of consciousness I bring to my work.

5. I am responsible for how I treat my body.

6. I am responsible for choosing my relationships.

7. I am responsible for the way I treat other people, animals, and the planet.

8. I am responsible for the meaning I give or fail to give to my existence.

9. I am responsible for my life—materially, emotionally, intellectually.

10. I am the chief causal agent in my life and behavior.

Some related PPR (positivity, personal responsibility) sayings:

- You can't worry about something if you are working to take care of it.

- You are what you think, eat, do, and practice.

- Everything you are and will be is a result of what is in your mind.

- If you want to evolve and grow rapidly, you must make your goals clear, sharp, and intense, and you must dwell on them constantly.

- Focus on what you want, not on what you don't want.

- The key to getting what you want is to be willing to do whatever is necessary.

- Determination and discipline are important for goal achievement—"Everything counts."

- Progress always involves risk.

- Whatever you think about over and over again grows into your reality.

- Success = goals; the mastery skill of success is the ability to set goals, create action plans, and carry those plans out.

- Failing is essential to success, as it is impossible to succeed without some failures along the way.

- Whatever leaves you feeling bad—do less of. Whatever leaves you feeling good—do more of.

- To achieve bigger goals, take smaller steps.

- Lie down and rest for a while.

- When you don't know what to say, try telling the truth.

- Life is a series of negotiations.

- Leave a margin—a margin of time, money, a margin of doubt.

- Less is more.

- Start the way you intend to finish.

- Strive for excellence, not perfection.

- Contentment is the new rich.

- Inner peace is the new success.

- Health is the new wealth.

- Kindness is the new cool.

On Finding Your Area of Excellence/Passion[56]

Where does your attention go? What are you interested in? What absorbs you?

Do this helpful Monthly Exercise (write the answers down)

1. What are the 5 things that you value most in life?

2. What are your 3 most important goals in life?

3. If you had only 6 months to live, how would you spend your time?

4. If you became an instant millionaire, what would you do differently than what you are doing today?

5. What have you always wanted to do, but have been afraid to attempt?

6. What sort of activities in life give you the greatest sense of importance?

7. If you knew you absolutely could not fail, what one great thing would you dare to dream?

---

56   www.authentichappiness.org (Martin Seligman's website)

Thriving in Transitions (which is all of life!)— Characteristics of Thrivers and Flourishers

- Self-awareness, receptivity, internal motivation, resilience, commitment to growth, proactive creation skills, experimentation, strong sense of purpose, flexible/adaptable, comfort with ambiguity, systems thinking, optimism, risk-taking

OTHER METHODS TO ASSIST WITH POSITIVITY AND PERSONAL RESPONSIBILITY

Meditation and Mindfulness[57]

Mindfulness meditation has been scientifically shown to help decrease anxiety and tension and increase gray matter in the brain when practiced regularly. It can also increase compassion, enhance focus, and improve sleep.

Meditation facilitates integration of information by allowing time for previously unrelated thoughts and feelings to interact. Being able to get in touch with one's deepest thoughts and feelings and providing time for them to regroup into new formations and combinations are important aspects of the creative process, as well as a way of relieving tension and promoting mental health.

---

57   Kabat-Zinn, J. *Mindfulness for Beginners: reclaiming the present moment and your life.* 2006

Contemplation, reflection, and self-nurturing are essential for mental health and can lead to increased personal and outer-world awareness and appreciation.

Meditation and Mindfulness—free resources (qualified psychotherapists, leaders)

Podcasts

- Meditation at the Hammer (hosted by UCLA, Mindfulness Awareness Research Centre)
- Spirit Rock Meditation Centre
- One Mind Meditation Podcast

YouTube and Blogs

- Positive Magazine
- Monday Meditations from Hay House

Spotify

- Guided Meditation
- Nature Sounds
- Focus and Concentration
- Multiple Playlists—Ambient Music

Practicing Intentional Simplicity[58,59] (balanced living)—Balance (the middleway) is a high virtue (but not the only virtue)

- Based on intentional (purposeful) simplicity (directness of expression, which is possible when there is no clutter to interfere with that expression).

A lifestyle approach, which is about:

- Analyzing what you want and how you want to live your life
- Making decisions that enhance quality of life
- The mindfulness with which we acquire and utilize money and goods
- Abundance vs scarcity
- Wholeness (both/and) vs duality (either/or)
- Thriving, not just surviving

It is not about:

- Doing without
- Deprivation
- Scarcity
- Dropping out

---

58   Dickinson, R. *Cut the Crap: How to Lead a Simpler Life*. SJG Publishing, UK. 2019

59   Layne, E. *The Minimalist Way: Minimalism Strategies to Declutter Your Life and Make Room for Joy*. Althea Press. 2019.

- What we have/don't have
- An absence of materialism

It is achieved by making decisions based on intentioned directions we want to pursue.

On anxiety, stress, and tensions (if severe, see a psychologist):

- Talk it out with close friends, family, trusted counsellors.
- Escape for a while—walk, short trip, reading, quiet time alone.
- Work off your anger—exercise, housework.
- Do something for others.
- Take one thing at a time; slow down.
- Shun the super-woman or super-man/super-person role.
- Go easy on your criticisms of yourself or others.
- Give other people a break—cooperate and collaborate more than you compete.
- Make yourself available—make an effort with people.
- Schedule your recreation.

On Living Better Emotionally & Developing Resilience, Grit and Hope[60]

These 7 steps can serve (to some degree) as life goals, if we seek to make the most of our own personalities.

1. Face reality.

2. Adapt to change—we must be resilient, adaptable, and strong.

3. Manage anxiety—manage your thoughts, words, and behaviour.

4. Give of yourself—every person needs a cause/mission/passion.

5. Be considerate and relate to other people sincerely and with integrity.

6. Curb hostility—direct it into creative/constructive outlets.

7. Learn to care—get out of yourself; become less self-centred.

Overcoming adversity and setbacks (the story of every human life):

1. Coping with stress, trauma, difficulties in a mindful, authentic way

2. Can be taught and learned

---

60   Duckworth, A. *Grit: The Power of Passion and Perseverance*. Collins. 2016.

3. Includes such factors as:

    a. Problem-solving skills (resourcefulness)

    b. Willingness to seek help

    c. Agency—the belief that they can help themselves (internal locus of control)

    d. Social support—have friends, family and others to connect with

    e. Spirituality—not connected to religion, but rather to the belief that all humans are connected to each other, and our connection is grounded in love and compassion

4. Other key factors in having grit include:

    a. Cultivating hope

    b. Practicing critical awareness

    c. Letting go of the need to feel and show invulnerability (in other words, being vulnerable and willing to experience pain and discomfort as common human conditions)—learning to tolerate and expect disappointment (being realistic)

5. Hope is not an emotion—it is a way of thinking or a cognitive process including:

    a. Goals—knowing that persistence and hard work are crucial

b. Pathways—plans to achieve goals, willingness to look at alternative ways (flexibility)

c. Agency (I can do this; I believe in myself)

d. Is a conscious choice

e. Can be taught and learned

On How to Be Healthy—exercise, healthy eating, sleep, personal self-care. Take care of your health now or you'll be taking care of your illness later.

- **Exercise - see *Handbook for Physical Activity* (Canada, UK and USA) for much more detail**

- **www.paguide.com (publication of Health Canada)**

Active Living as a way of life (essentially move more and sit less whenever possible), endurance, flexibility and strength—try to do these 3-7 days per week but mix them up in whatever combination/permutation that works for you. Variety is the spice of life—do what you enjoy and you are more likely to continue. Different countries have different guidelines/guides but in general, regular daily activity (accumulation of 150 minutes moderate activity or 75 minutes vigorous weekly minimum) is required to have a healthy body and prevent sedentary-related chronic diseases such as type 2 diabetes, obesity, heart disease, and high blood pressure.

- **Healthy Eating - see Canada's Food Guide, UK and USA www.Canada.ca/FoodGuide (publication of Health Canada)**

  If you'd like a particular guide to follow, the Canadian, American, and British food guides (most countries have their own, reflecting the tastes and preferences of their own population) are good starting points; essentially for most people, a diet high in plant foods such as vegetables, fruits, whole grains, and smaller amounts of protein foods (nuts, seeds, beans, lentils, dairy, eggs, fish, poultry, and meats) is recommended. Unprocessed is optimal. Limiting alcohol, saturated fat, sodium, and high sugar and low nutrient (empty calorie) foods is recommended. Work with a registered dietitian if you need help with a plan that is tailored to you specifically. Diet is equally as important as physical activity for prevention of chronic diseases such as type 2 diabetes, heart disease, high blood pressure, and some cancers.

- **Sleep**
  www.nih.gov (National Institute of Health)
  www.mayoclinic.org>sleep (Mayo Clinic)
  www.healthysleep.med.harvard.edu>tips (Harvard Medical Education)
  www.sleepfoundation.org

Adequate quality and quantity of sleep has been shown to be critical for mental and emotional well-being, as well as prevention of chronic diseases (obesity can increase with poor/inadequate sleep, which can lead to poor health outcomes such as type 2 diabetes, heart disease, and high blood pressure). There has been much written on sleep hygiene, but basically it includes: turning off all electronic devices two hours prior to sleeping, creating a calming bedtime ritual (quiet), keeping the same basic hours of going to bed and getting up (not possible for everyone), not eating right before going to bed, limiting caffeine (to before two p.m.) and alcohol. Alcohol can interfere with depth of sleep and cause interrupted and low-quality sleep.

Personal self-care[61]

- Don't do things that will make you sick!

- Don't think thoughts that will make you sad/mad/bad.

- Don't spend time with people that who aren't good for you (toxic people).

- Don't indulge in out-of-control behaviour.

- Do ½ to 1-hour mindfulness meditation daily to focus on these five things:

  - Knowing yourself

  - Discovering what makes you happy

---

61   Brown, B. *The Gifts of Imperfection*. Hazelden Publishing. 2010.

- Learning to ask for what you want

- Accepting what can't be changed

- Realizing that you will change, and others will change (not to be feared)

- Keep a journal/paper handy to write down notes about the above.

Other ways to nurture yourself:

- Limit complaining (it does not make you or others feel better).

- Explore lifestyle changes that might help you manage your life better.

- Practice humility—recognize that everyone is doing the best they can in their lives.

- Decide to make good-enough decisions—perfectionistic tendencies can lead to increased anxiety and feelings of being out-of-control. Doing something is better than doing nothing.

- Finding solutions gives you agency, and positively changes your perception of the world.

- By keeping a gratitude journal, you increase the feel-good brain neurotransmitters serotonin and dopamine.

- Be as involved in your community as you can:
    - Participate in schools, service, and sports clubs.

- Government—inform yourself; every citizen *is the government*—your vote is important.
- Be generous with your praise, time, and money.

GLOSSARY

DEFINITIONS (OXFORD DICTIONARY) & TIMELINES

Age of Enlightenment (Age of Reason) (c. 1600-1800)— Intellectual and philosophical developments took place that were crucial in bringing progress to humankind. Isaac Newton's *Principa Mathematica* was a key enlightenment work. Other key people include: Francis Bacon, Immanuel Kant, John Locke, Jean-Jacques Rousseau, and Voltaire.

Agnosticism—Belief that we don't know whether or not a god/gods exist.

Atheism—Belief in no god/gods.

Balance—The concept that there is a "middle ground" between two extremes or two opposite forces (whether in politics, economics, health); nothing in excess; one of the main recommendations in this book as a virtue to aspire to.

Big Bang Theory—The leading explanation of how the universe began. About 13.82 billion years ago, the universe expanded from a subatomic particle (a singularity), which was in inflationary space; From mathematical formulas and models and from a phenomenon that scientists can measure (or "see" the "echo" of), known as "cosmic microwave background," scientists can show that the universe did expand, and therefore, the birth of the universe can be explained. The cosmic microwave background has been observed on many space missions (repeatable observations); in addition, at LIGO (Laser Interferometer Gravitational-Wave Observatory), gravitational waves have been confirmed on multiple occasions. These are important with respect to movements and collisions of black holes. Another way of putting it: about fourteen billion years ago, there was nothing and nowhere. Then due to a random fluctuation in an empty void, a universe exploded into existence. The subatomic particle (the singularity) inflated to an incredible size almost instantaneously. Negative pressure (vacuum energy) drove the expansion. Ethan Siegal, PhD, physicist, educator, and science writer, has subsequently updated the Big Bang singularity to explain that the singularity itself arose from an *inflationary energy state*, so prior to the actual Big Bang, the universe was filled with energy inherent to space itself, causing a rapid exponential expansion that stretched the universe flat and gave it the same properties everywhere with small amplitude quantum fluctuations.(Christian, David: Origin Story & Harari, Yuval: Sapiens)

Constitution—A set of principles and rules that define the structure and extent of an entity (government, state, province, nation).

Charter of Human Rights and Freedoms—Entrenched within an entity's constitution; designed to unify all people of a nation/state/province/entity around a set of principles that embody those rights.

Cult—A system of religious belief; devotion to a person (example, Jesus) or thing (example, God).

Deism—Is a philosophy, not a religion (there is no holy book); the belief that God created the universe, but remains apart from it and permits his creation to administer itself through natural laws; belief that there is a god but not revelation.

Delusion—A false belief or opinion; a hallucination.

Dogma or doctrine(s)—Principles and beliefs put forward by some authority, especially the church/political party, to be accepted as true without question.

Economics—The science concerned with the production and consumption/use of goods and services; the financial aspects of something.

Ethics—Moral philosophy and principles; rules provided by an external source (a workplace "Code of Conduct," for example) concerning right and wrong behaviour.

Evidence—Proofs that explain facts.

Evolution—The natural process by which living things change gradually (natural selection) and rapidly (horizontal gene transfer) into different forms; based on proofs of biogeography (common African ancestor), transitional fossils, embryology, molecular biology, existence of vestigial organs.

Existentialism (Personal Responsibility)—A philosophical theory emphasizing that people are responsible for their own actions, and are free to choose their development and destiny; insists that each individual, through their own actions, must create his/her own meaning in life, and that there is no grand meaning to the world other than that which we give it; a very liberating idea—we can create our own meaning.

Faith—Trust or reliance; belief in religious doctrine.

Freethought/Freethinkers—A viewpoint that holds that positions regarding truth should be formed only on the basis of logic, reason, and empiricism as opposed to authority, tradition, revelation, or dogma.

Humanism—A non-religious philosophy based on liberal human values (tolerance and open-mindedness) with the belief in leading moral and purposeful lives; A VERY POSITIVE life stance on how to approach personal, community, and global health; values include democracy, rule of law, equality, and human rights.

Ideals of the Enlightenment—Centred on REASON as the primary source of knowledge: Ideals include progress, tolerance, fraternity, constitutional government, freedom from tyranny, and the separation of church and state.

Illusion—Something that a person wrongly supposes to exist; a false belief about the nature of something.

Metaphysics—A branch of philosophy that deals with existence, truth and knowledge; abstract or subtle thought; theoretical.

Morals—Formed from an individual's values (what a person considers right or wrong behaviour).

Middle Ages (aka: The **Dark Ages**) (c. 5c-1500s AD)—This medieval period of European History began with the demise of the western Roman Empire (the "classical era"), and ended with the Age of Discovery/Renaissance (rebirth). It is known for mass migrations of different tribes throughout Europe and Northern Africa. Christianity was a new cult that tried to convert pagans. Around 1000 AD, human population increased greatly due to improvements in agriculture and trade routes. There was also a "medieval warm period" (climate change) at this time that allowed crop yields to increase. Civilization was structured mostly around the feudal system, in which serfs and villagers worked the land for overlords/nobles. Intellectual life was "scholasticism"—a philosophy emphasizing the marriage of faith to reason. Universities were established. Toward the end of the period, there were many wars, plagues (the black death; bubonic plague in the fourteenth century), and famine, which significantly decreased the population. Peasants continued to revolt against the landowners, while technological improvements were starting to transform Europe. (Christian, David: *Origin Story*)

Naturalism—A belief in the natural laws of nature; including biology, biochemistry, chemistry, math, and physics (and the relations between all of them); To many scientists, the combined laws of gravity, relativity, quantum physics, and a few other scientific rules can explain everything that ever happened, or will ever happen in our known universe.

Philosophy—A system of ideas concerning the search, by logical reasoning, for understanding of the basic truths and principles of the universe, life, morals, and the human perception and understanding of these principles for the conduct of life.

Pluralism—A form of society with many minority groups and cultures.

Racism—Belief in the superiority of a particular race; prejudice based on this; antagonism towards peoples of other races.

Realist—A person whose ideas are based on facts, not on ideals or illusion.

Reason—The capacity for consciously making sense of things; establishing and verifying facts; applying logic; and changing or justifying practices, institutions, and beliefs based on new and existing information.

Religion—A system of beliefs in and worship of a supernatural, controlling power, especially God or gods.

Scam—A fraudulent trick.

Secularism—Not involving religion; concerned with the natural (fact-based) world, not the supernatural; a conscious, non-spiritual, rational ideology for social betterment in the here and now.

Spiritual—Non-material and non-observable concerns; about a person's relationship with the transcendent questions that humans have; may or may not involve a relationship with a "god."

Superstition/Supernatural—A belief that events can be influenced by forces outside of nature; a belief that is held by a number of people but without foundation or evidence.

Transcendent—Going beyond the limits of ordinary experience; (of God)—existing beyond the material universe.

Values—Standards or principles considered important in life.

Xenophobia—Hatred or distrust of foreigners or "others".

Note to reader—I had to limit the scope of this book's contents to (mostly) the Western world. This is not to negate in any way the important contributions of the other continents (Asia, Africa, South America, and Australia) but suffice it to say that there are many recurrent themes running through the development of each of these continents' countries that parallel the Western world although they may be at differing stages in their development.

HAPPIER HUMANS REFERENCES & RECOMMENDED READING LIST

By **Steven Pinker** (UK, USA, Canadian-born; psychologist, prominent author)

Enlightenment Now. The Case for Reason, Science, Humanism, and Progress

The Better Angels of our Natures

The Language Instinct

How the Mind Works

The Blank Slate

The Stuff of Thought

By **David Christian** (professor, pioneering the field of Big History)

Origin Story

By **Yuval Noah Harari** (Israeli public intellectual, professor, writer)

Sapiens: A Brief History of Humankind

By **A. C. Grayling** (UK, professor of philosophy)

The God Argument: The Case Against Religion and For Humanism

The Good Book: A Humanist Bible

By **Victor Stenger** (USA, particle physicist, University of Hawaii)

God: The Failed Hypothesis: How Science Shows God Does Not Exist

The New Atheism: Taking a Stand for Science and Reason

God and the Multiverse: Humanity's Expanding View of the Cosmos

Not by Design: The Origin of the Universe

Physics and Psychics: The Search for a World Beyond the Senses

The Fallacy of Fine Tuning: Why the Universe is Not Designed for Us

God the Folly of Faith: The Incompatibility of Science and Religion

By **Christopher Hitchens** (UK, USA, writer, historian)

The Portable Atheist

God is Not Great: How Religion Poisons Everything

By **Stephen Hawking** (UK, Professor of Physics)

The Universe in a Nutshell

The Theory of Everything

Brief Answers to Big Questions

God Created the Integers: The Mathematical Breakthroughs that Changed History

By **Richard Dawkins** (UK, Oxford University)

Outgrowing God: A Beginner's Guide

The God Delusion

The Selfish Gene

The Blind Watchmaker

By **Daniel Dennett** (USA, professor of Philosophy, Tufts University)

Caught in the Pulpit: Leaving Belief Behind

Breaking the Spell: Religion as a Natural Phenomenon

Darwin's Dangerous Idea

Consciousness Explained

By **Sam Harris** (USA, neural science for belief)

The End of Faith

Letter to a Christian Nation

The Moral Landscape

By **E. O. Wilson** (Harvard professor)

On Human Nature

The Future of Life

By **Bertrand Russell** (UK, logician, mathematician, philosopher, historian, political activist, social critic, writer)

Why I am Not a Christian

By **Michael Shermer** – (*Skeptic Magazine* founding publisher, science writer and lecturer)

Skeptic—Viewing the World with a Rational Eye

The Moral Arc: How Science and Reason lead humanity toward truth, justice, and freedom

The Believing Brain: From Ghosts & Gods to Conspiracies & Politics—How we construct beliefs and reinforce them as truths

Why Darwin Matters: Evolution and the Case Against Intelligent Design

The Science of Good and Evil: Why People Cheat and Lie, Share and Care, and Follow the Golden Rule

Why People Believe Weird Things

By **Ayaan Ali Hirsi** (vocal critic of Islam, writer, politician)

Infidel

The Caged Virgin

Nomad

By **Philip Pullman** (UK writer and social critic, public intellectual)

His Dark Materials (trilogy)

The Good Man Jesus & the Scoundrel Christ

By **Patricia Churchland** (Canadian professor working at UCSD Professor of Philosophy)

The Computational Brain

Brain Trust: What Neuroscience Tells Us about Morality

Neurophilosophy: Toward a Unified Science of the Mind-Brain

By **Lawrence Krauss** (theoretical physicist and cosmologist, University of Arizona, Yale, Case Western professor)
A Universe from Nothing
The Unbelievers (movie)

By **David Sloane Wilson** (USA, Binghamton University Distinguished Professor)
Darwin's Cathedral

By **Dan Barker** (USA)—former protestant minister
Godless, the Good Atheist

By **Paul Kurtz** (NY, USA) aka the Father of Secular Humanism
Humanist Manifesto 2000
What is Secular Humanism?
Living Without Religion
The Transcendental Temptation

By **Peter Atkins** (UK, professor of chemistry University of Oxford)
Creation Revisited
Four Laws that Drive the Universe
On Being

By **Jerry Coyne** (professor at University of Chicago in ecology and evolution)
Why Evolution is True

Faith vs Fact: Why Science and Religion are Incompatible

By **Kai Nielson** (Canada, professor of philosophy, University of Calgary)
Ethics Without God
Atheism and Philosophy

By **Peter Singer** (professor of bioethics at Princeton University)
Unsanctifying Human Life

By **Susan Jacoby** (USA public intellectual, writer)
Freethinkers: A History of American Secularism
The Age of American Unreason

By **William Lobdell** (former religion reporter and Evangelical Christian)
Losing My Religion

By **Jennifer Michael Hecht** (professor, writer)
The End of the Soul: Doubt - A History
The Happiness Myth

By **John W. Loftus**
Why I Became an Atheist—A Former Preacher Rejects Christianity

Edited by **S.T. Joshi** (scholar, writer)
The Original Atheists; First Thoughts on Non-Belief
The Unbelievers

The Agnostic Reader
God's Defenders
Atheism: A Reader

By **Andre Comte-Sponville**, (French philosopher, translated by Nancy Huston)
The Little Book of Atheist Spirituality

By **Kerry S. Walters** (USA, Professor of Philosophy, Gettysburg College)
Atheism: A Guide for the Perplexed

Edited by: **Russell Blackford** & **Udo Schuklenk**

50 Voices of Disbelief: Why We are Atheists

Edited by: **Linda Woodhead, Paul Fletcher, Hiroko Kawanami, David Smith**
Religions in the Modern World

By **Reza Aslan** (USA-Iranian, scholar of religious studies, writer and tv host)
Zealot: The Life and Times of Jesus of Nazareth
God: A Human History

By **David Quammen** (USA, science, nature and travel writer)
The Tangled Tree

By **Phil Zuckerman** (USA, professor of Sociology, Claremont College)

What it Means to be Moral

Living the Secular Life

Society Without God

Faith No More

By **Greg Epstein** (Humanist Chaplain at Harvard and MIT)

Good Without God

By **Richard Wilkinson** and **Kate Pinkett** (UK professors, social epidemiologists)

The Inner Level—How more equal societies reduce stress, restore sanity and improve everyone's well-being

By **Hannah Critchlow** (UK, neuroscientist at Cambridge University)

The Science of Fate

By **Jack Gorman** (Oxford University, psychiatrist)

Denying to the Grave—why we ignore facts that will save us

By **Susan Blackmore** (UK professor, writer)

The Meme Machine

Consciousness—An Introduction

By **Dr. Hugo Mercier** (cognitive psychologist, France) and Dan Sperber
The Enigma of Reason
The Knowledge Illusion

By **Elizabeth Kolbert** (*New Yorker* staff writer since 1999)
Book: *The Sixth Extinction: An Unnatural History (2015 Pulitzer for non-fiction)*

By **Brian Boone (USA)**
Ethics 101

By **Alain de Botton** (French writer)
Religion for Atheists: A Non-believer's Guide to the Uses of Religion

By **Christopher Hitchens, Richard Dawkins, Sam Harris and Daniel Dennett**
The Four Horsemen: The Conversation that Sparked an Atheist Revolution

By **Eric Maisel** (USA, psychotherapist)
The Atheist's Way: Living Well Without Gods

By **National Geographic**
Essential Visual History of World Mythology

By **Jimmy Carter** (Former President of the USA, humanitarian)
A Call to Action—Women, Religion, Violence, and Power

By **Brene Brown** (professor of sociology, University of Houston, writer, podcast host)
The Gifts of Imperfection

By **Angela Duckworth** (USA, academic, popular science writer)
Grit

By **Marc Brackett** (USA, research psychologist, Yale)
Permission to Feel

By **Martin Seligman** (USA, psychology professor, writer)
*Flourish: A Visionary New Understanding of Happiness
    and Well-being*
*Authentic Happiness: Using the new positive psychology to realize
    your potential for lasting fulfillment*

By **Jon Kabat-Zinn** (USA, professor emeritus of medicine, University of Massachusetts, founder of MBSR – mindfulness based stress reduction)
*Mindfulness for Beginners: Reclaiming the present moment—and
    your life.*
Mindfulness Meditation for Everyday Life

OTHER REFERENCE SOURCES—WEBSITES AND BLOGS

- Humanists International (www.humanists.international) based in London, UK, maintains a presence at the UN Human Rights Council in Geneva, within the United Nations system

- Humanists Canada (Humanist Association of Canada)

  - A registered charity with a mandate to promote the separation of religion from public policy, and foster the development of reason, compassion, and critical thinking for all Canadians

- The American Humanist Society

- British Humanist Association (has excellent resources for teachers)

- Many countries have a humanist organization

- American Association for the Advancement of Science www.aaas.org (Science magazine)

- thehumanist.com

- International Humanist News—email newsletter

- Gapminder.org

- Free Inquiry Magazine publications

- Centre for Inquiry

- Edge.org

Human Rights

- Amnesty International

- United Nations Website

- Humanist Manifesto 2000: A Call for Planetary Humanism

Environment and Climate

- The Ecologist magazine/Resurgence & Ecologist

- Theecologist.org

- Environment and the new Humanism—by O. E. Wilson

- www.unesco.org

SOME MORE HUMANIST QUOTES

Humanism is the belief that we can live good lives without religious or superstitious beliefs.
(British Humanist Association, 2003)

The crucial test of ethical values is whether they apply to strangers and those afar, not just in our midst.
(Bernard Crick, *Essays on Citizenship*, 2000)

Do not do to others what you would not like for yourself.
(Confucius, *Analects*, C 500 BCE)

*Repay injury with justice, and kindness
with kindness.*
(Confucius, *Analects,* c 500 BCE)

*As man advances in civilization, and small tribes are
united into larger communities, the simplest reason
would tell each individual that he ought to extend his
social instincts and sympathies to all the members
of the same nation, though personally unknown to
him. This point once reached, there is only artificial
(religious) barrier to prevent his sympathies
extending to the men of all nations and races.*
(Charles Darwin, *The Descent of Man,* 1871)

*Of all the means by which wisdom ensures happiness
throughout life, by far the most important is the
possession of friendship.*
(Epicurus, *Principle Doctrines,* c.300 BCE)

*I do not want my house to be walled in on all sides
and my windows stuffed. I want the cultures of
all lands to be blown about my house as freely as
possible…But I refuse to be blown off my feet by any.*
(Mahatma Gandhi, 1869-1948)

No one was ever injured by the truth; but he who
persists in self-deception and ignorance is injured.
(Marcus Aurelius, 121-80 CE), *Meditations*

A wise man proportions his belief to the evidence.
(David Hume, *An Enquiry Concerning Human*
Understanding, 1748)

It is wrong, always, everywhere, and for anyone, to
believe anything upon insufficient evidence.
W. K. Clifford, The *Ethics of Belief,* 1877

It is wrong for a man to say that he is certain of
the objective truth of any proposition unless he
can produce evidence which logically justifies
the certainty.
T. H. Huxley, *Agnosticism and Christianity,* 1889

Rationalism is an attitude of readiness to listen to
contrary arguments and to learn from experience…
of admitting that "I may be wrong, and you may be
right, and, by an effort, we may get nearer the truth
Karl Popper, *The Open Society and its Enemies,* 1945

How much reverence can you have for a Supreme Being who finds it necessary to include such phenomena as phlegm and tooth decay in His divine system of creation?
Joseph Heller, *Catch 22*

Religion: a daughter of Hope and Fear, explaining to Ignorance the nature of the Unknowable.
Ambrose Bierce, 1842-1914

God is a hypothesis, and as such, stands in need of proof; the onus probandi (burden of proof) rests on the theist.
Percy Bysshe Shelley, *Note on the Queen Mab*; a Philosophical Poem, 1813

If the gods have the will to remove evil and cannot, then they are not all-powerful. If they are neither able nor willing, they are neither all-powerful nor benevolent. If they are both able and willing to annihilate evil, why does it exist?
Epicurus, c 300 BCE

Faith: a firm belief for which there is no evidence.
Bertrand Russell, *Human Society in Ethics and Politics*, 1954

A good world needs knowledge, kindness, and courage; it does not need a regretful hankering after the past of a fettering of the free intelligence by the words uttered long ago by ignorant men.
Bertrand Russell, *Why I am Not a Christian*, 1927

People who are always praising the past, and especially the time of faith as best, ought to go live in the Middle Ages, and be burnt at the stake as witches and sages.
Stevie Smith, poet

The gods we make in our own image are tribal gods. They tell you how very, very little you should tolerate outsiders, who are less favoured of the Lord. Amazingly, there are no recorded cases of the holy man going up the mountain and finding out that it's the others who are right. It always turns out that God wants unbelievers to suffer, and what could be more noble than to help him a little? When religion rules, toleration disappears, for you cannot cherish the verdict of death to the infidels, yet also tolerate those who disagree—for those are the very same infidels.
Simon Blackburn, 2004

I was not and was conceived.
I loved and did a little work.
I am not and grieve not.
W. K. Clifford

The wise man neither rejects life nor fears death…
just as he does not necessarily choose the largest
amount of food, but rather, the pleasantest food, so
he prefers not the longest time, but the most pleasant.
Epicurus, *Letter to Menoeceus* (c 300 BCE)

Death is nothing to us; for after our bodies have
been dissolved by death they are without sensation,
and that which lacks sensation is nothing to us. And
therefore, a right understanding of death makes
mortality enjoyable, not because it adds to an infinite
span of time, but because it takes away the craving
for immortality.
Epicurus, *Principal Doctrines*, c 300 BCE

SOME OTHER NOTABLE SECULAR HUMANISTS

This is a very limited list; includes many Nobel prize winners and laureates.

Dr. Henry Morgentaler	J. Bentham
Stephen Fry	Steve Wozniak
Steve Allen	Albert Einstein
June Callwood	Gene Roddenberry
Leonard Bernstein	Paul D Boyer
Linus Pauling	Margaret Sanger
Ralph Alpher	Albert Ellis
Margaret Atwood	James Randi
Niels Bohr	Jacob Bronowski
Aaron Copland	Jonas Salk
N. Al-Rodhan	Francis Crick
Sue Rodriquez	Andrei Sakharov
Johannes Brahms	Mary Calderone
Henry Taube	Edward O. Wilson
PW Anderson	Murray Gell-Mann
Dr. Robert Buckman	Erwin Schrodinger
Charlie Chaplin	V. F. Turchin
Abraham Maslow	Albert Schweitzer
AJ Ayer	Aldous Huxley
John Ralston Saul	B. F. Skinner
J. R. Oppenheimer	Brian Cox

Joyce Carol Oates	D. R. Herschbach
Julian Huxley	Pervez Hoodbhoy
Peter Ustinov	Harry Kroto
John Dewey	Bill Maher
Salman Rushdie	Ashley Montague
Penn Jillete	P. Z. Myers
Rebecca Goldstein	Jawaharlal Nehru
Paul Dirac	Erwin Neher
Richard Branson	Carl R. Rogers
Norman Lear	Joseph Rotblat
Betty Friedan	Neil deGrasse Tyson
Matt Dillahunty	Bill Nye
Ian McKewan	Nikola Tesla
Walt Whitman	Cenk Uygur
Jerome I. Friedman	Ramswaroop Verma
Ann Dunham	Ibn Warraq
Martin Amis	James D Watson
John Lennon	Faye Wattleton
Barbara Ehrenreich	Steven Weinberg
Umberto Eco	Gloria Steinem
Phillip Roth	Ted Turner
Charles M. Schulz	
Greg Graffin	
H. A. Hauptman	
Katharine Hepburn	

CPSIA information can be obtained
at www.ICGtesting.com
Printed in the USA
BVHW090148021120
592311BV00001B/1

9 781525 565908